Influence and Negotiations:

The Philosophy of Systemic Thinking

Jon-Arild Johannessen

Copyright © 2016 Jon-Arild Johannessen

All rights reserved.

ISBN-13:
978-1537352664

ISBN-10:
1537352660

DEDICATION

To my wife

CONTENTS

DEDICATION iii

ACKNOWLEDGMENTS vi

Chapter 1 The negotiation context 7
    Introduction 7
    Developing a model 12
        Problem definition 12
        Information processes 14
        Situation framing 16
    Problem definition 18
        Context 19
        Systemic structuring 22
    Information 24
        Choosing information type 28
    Framing 30
        The value basis 30
    Conclusion 36
    References 37

Chapter 2 Influence 45
    Introduction 45
        Interpreter 53
        Cognitive processes 53
        Cognitive principles 57
        Heuristic mechanisms 66
    Message 71
        Information exchange (information sharing) 72
        Information analysis 73
        The choice of information type 75
    The speaker 76
        Characteristic features of the speaker 76

Conclusion 79
    Practical implications 79

Theoretical implications 81

References 82

Chapter 3 Prospect theory in negotiations: Influencing the Situation 92
Introduction 92
Literature review: Decision-making under uncertainty 94
Literature review: Framing 99
Literature review: Heuristic assessments 102
Specific measures that management can implement 107
  Decision-making under uncertainty 107
  Framing 108
  Heuristic assessments 110
Conclusion 111

References 112

Chapter 4 Mastering influence and negotiation 117
Introduction 117
Self-image 119
  Adaptability and self-regulation 127
Personal strength and powers of endurance 131
Conclusion 138

References 140

Chapter 5 Attitude change in Negotiations 149
Introduction 149
How attitudes change through how we think 156
How attitudes change through what we say 159
How attitudes change through what we do 167
Conclusion 175
References 178

Chapter on concepts 191

Index 237

Jon-Arild Johannessen

ACKNOWLEDGMENTS

To all my student through thirty years

Chapter 1 The negotiation context

Introduction

Putnam (1985:237) says that "Research on information management----- is sparse" in a negotiation perspective. This chapter is an attempt to bridge this knowledge gap. Our approach synthesises grounded and middle range theories related to information processes and negotiations. The model developed (fig. 1) in this chapter should provide a foundation for the empirical study of information management related to negotiations.

The main question we try to answer in this chapter is: How can we change a negotiation context from a win-loose situation to a win-win situation?

By information management is here meant the study of external and internal information and communication processes in systems.

By information is here meant the difference in a message conducive to the perception of a difference relative to previous knowledge, or with

Bateson (1972: 272) "the difference which makes the difference".

By communication is here meant the exchange of a message between two or more parties. By knowledge we here mean distinctions serving purpose. Based on this definition of knowledge we also state that it is when distinctions operate on information in a systematising and structuring way that knowledge is being developed.

With these three definitions of information, communication and knowledge, we have linked the three entities to a coherent system.

Conflicts (disagreements, disputes etc.) are a common phenomenon in the social universe. In order to resolve conflicts, there are several procedures, e.g. tradition, rules, rituals, court rooms, markets and negotiations. Negotiations represent a special type of conflict solutions according to Putnam (1985: 129).

What is negotiation? There is no unambiguous definition of the concept. We shall look at some definitions which have been used, and then try to synthesise the concept. Bazerman and Lewick (1983: 7) say that when two or more parties in the same organisation or in different ones make decisions, and they have different preferences, they negotiate. Negotiation according to this definition is linked to organisations and decisions. This has later been emphasised by Bazerman (1994: 123).

Negotiations can also be seen as being characterised by the exchange of proposals and counter-proposals as a means to achieve satisfactory resolutions to a reciprocal problem, according to Putnam (1985: 129). With Putnam negotiations are not necessarily linked to organisations, but rather to a general way of solving a common problem.

Rubin and Brown (1975: 2) focus on their definition of the importance of the information process. They also underline the importance of looking at negotiations as a process, where the parties must give and take in order to reach a solution. Carnevale and Isen (1986: 1) also link negotiations to decisions and differences in preferences, while at the same time underlining the process perspective in their definition.

Our comprehension is that all the angles of incidence to the concept negotiation mentioned above, can be synthesised by saying that negotiations are related to disagreement or conflict, where there are differences in terms of perception among/between the parties. The parties are further in various ways related to each other, and participate in a voluntary process aimed at resolving the conflict. The conflict will always demonstrate a development testifying to the formation of a pattern in the social interaction between the parties. The various conflicts make up various contexts, and it is essential in order to reach effective solutions, to determine what type of context is dominant. To put it more concretely, we could say that a negotiation situation occurs when two or more parties are involved in a conflict of interest pertaining to resources or a problem, and where the parties engage in a voluntary relationship to resolve existing conflicts. The parties involved can meet directly or through a third party. This being said, we regard negotiations are a phenomenon which covers most aspects of every-day life. They stretch from the personal level to the international society.

It is three theories which historically have dominated research on negotiation, according to Putnam (1985: 130); game theory, negotiation theory and institutional economy. Game theory has been difficult to transfer from "laboratory experiment" to real field studies aimed at the study or predication of negotiation behaviour, according to Kochan (1980). Negotiation theory focuses on the actions of the parties, i.e. proposals and counter-proposals. They try to find how proposals and counter-proposals work in negotiations. But in any case the models tend to be abstract, theoretical and difficult to apply in negotiations. They are further unable to incorporate experience acquired in the actual negotiation process, says Gulliver (1979). The institutional theory left the game-theoretical paradigm and quantitative techniques. Instead it focuses on historical and empirical analyses, according to Kochan (1980:132). Practical cases constitute the centre of attention. As a consequence of one-dimensional case-approach, this angle of incidence only to a minor extent would contribute to theory development in the field (Kochan, 1980).

Gulliver (1979) argues that all three perspectives preclude organisational rules, norms, routine, basic notions, the distribution of power and the importance of external factors in negotiations. According to Gulliver (1979), what is needed is non-economic models analysing negotiations by focusing on processes and organisational contexts.

Process studies are based on concrete negotiations from every-day life. Instead of using rationality as a basic premise, this approach presupposes limited and diverse skills on the part of the negotiators, both in terms of receiving, and reacting to messages from their opposite party. Two main models are fundamental in the process-oriented angle of incidence: cognitive models, focusing on how future expectations influence the negotiation situation (Gulliver, 1979), and learning models, focusing on how experiences form rules, norms and behavioural patterns for future actions (Cross, 1977).

Rubin and Brown (1975) underline the importance of information processes in negotiation situations, and regards the exchange of information as the essential entity in the research context. Also Strauss (1978), with his concept of "negotiated order", focuses on the environment and the social context. The difference from Hochan is that Strauss emphasises the interpretation on the part of the actors that the context is an essential element. For Strauss negotiated order is equivalent to goals, regulations, and routines being continually the object for negotiation in an organisation. In this manner negotiation is a continuous process in an organisation where order is established and re-established by means of the negotiation process.

The part of the negotiation process which analyses social interactions as a communication process is ignored by the classic perspective, according to Putnam (1985a:236). Research on communication and negotiation focuses on "formal event in which the opposition of goals and values is pursued, it stresses interdependence between disputants and highlights social interaction as the essence of conflict enactment and management" (Putnam and Pool, 1987: 573).

Today it appears that five perspectives seem to be dominant in a negotiation context, i.e. game theory, negotiation theory, institutional economy, the process perspective and communication. Our contribution is mainly linked to the process and communication perspective, but also draws inspiration from other perspectives related to information management. We also make connections to the behavioural focus around which Pruitt's (1981;191) research revolves.

In the following section the main constructs in the general model are developed. Following that, the model is presented. We will then (part III) discuss the abstract variables which constitute the main constructs in the model. Several research propositions mainly focusing the transition from a win-loose context to a win-win context are presented.

Developing a model.

In the previous section we briefly described the different perspectives of negotiations. These streams focused on somewhat different aspects of negotiations. In this section we rely on these insights to provide the basis of a general model of information management in negotiations. The resulting model is depicted in figure 1. The organising idea behind the model is that the parts in a negotiation have to define their problems (Problem definition), get information about the problem (Information processes), and frame the negotiation situation (Situation framing). Underlying these constructs are the underpinnings identified from the research streams in negotiations.

Problem definition

The purpose of problem definition is to get a complete survey of the boundaries to be drawn, the context to which the problem belongs or has belonged, and the relationship between the individual components of the problem and the complete structure (systemic structuring).

A situation will in its consequence develop according to our definition of it, according to Thomas (1928). This is the so-called Thomas theorem, first used by Merton (1949). How we define a situation will greatly influence our choice of action in the situation in question.

We have made a deliberate distinction in the model (fig. 1) between problem definition and situation framing in order to differentiate between problem definition as a cognitive category and situation framing as an action category.

One important aspect of problem definition is that our picture of the outside world is critical to our way of defining a problem, situation etc. What is important to notice in this connection, is that we as observers are a part of this social environment, and that we thus influence the situation by our way of defining the problem or situation. We are thus not outside the problem, looking at it like an observer. In negotiation situations, like in social interaction in general, we are always a part of what we are observing. This distinction is critical. We are not observers of social reality. We are a part of what we observe, and it is this fact that makes problem definition extremely difficult. If we are not conscious of this, we will often find ourselves in a conflict situation with the expectations towards our object of observation. Social reality cannot be created in the same manner as a chair being created by a carpenter. We are a part of what is created, and are thus subject to change in the course of this process. There is mutual interaction between us as observers of social reality and the social reality in question.

Any problem in a negotiation estimates a borderline to another problem, but all problems are part of the superior negotiating situation. How we structure a problem and where we draw the boundaries for a problem, thus seem to affect the total negotiating situation.

Another point related to problem structuring is the attempt to uncover various knowledge categories dominating a negotiating situation. One way of structuring knowledge is to make distinctions between explicit knowledge, tacit knowledge and hidden knowledge.

Explicit knowledge is here regarded as the part of knowledge which can be verbally relayed to others in the form of information.

The tacit part of knowledge, says Polanyi (1962), is the part linked to our skills, which poses difficulties in terms of communication by means of language, e.g. to explain to others how other people's glances are to be interpreted in a negotiating situation.

Hidden knowledge is here defined as the part of knowledge which structures our premises, suppositions, preconditions and motives. The fact that this part of knowledge is hidden, makes it difficult for us to acquire insight into what factors will determine our actions or attitudes, e.g. in a negotiating situation. If this part of knowledge should remain more or less hidden from us, conflicts might easily occur, without our knowledge as to why and how they are created.

We find support for the concept hidden knowledge in Schutz' (1990, Vol. 1 and 2.) "epoche" concept.

The authentically dialogue, i.e. where honesty is pursued in relation to oneself as well as the other party, will, among other things, make parts of tacit and hidden knowledge accessible for communication. If this does not happen we will during the structuring of a problem not be fully aware of premises and suppositions affecting our definitions and problem demarcation in a negotiation situation. The problem may then easily be defined differently and lead to a different outcome, compared to a situation where complete awareness of hidden knowledge has been reached.

Information processes

The purpose of information processes in a negotiation situation is here regarded as: exchange of information, analysis of information for the purpose of bringing about the desired result and choice of information type.

The basis for the selection of information processes is found in Miller's

(1978) theory.

The connection between communication and information can be expresses by saying that the smallest unit in a communication unit is a message. A message can be understood and divided in three different parts. Firstly, it is the information part itself. It is the contents one tries to communicate to the other party. But the message also consists of a relationship part and an hierarchy part (Watzlawick et. al., 1967). The relation part says something about our relationship to the person we transmit information to or receive information from. The hierarchy part expresses where the person transmitting or receiving information is located in terms of status and social standing in society. In order to fully understand a message, it is therefore essential to be aware of the three constituents which the message consists of.

When a person utters a message, and we then interpret it, a lot of the information acquired is inherent in our relationship to the person uttering the message. Another way of putting this, is that there is a hierarchical structure in all communication processes, which, among other things, has to do with confidence, the type of relationship existing between the parties, their history, value bias etc. This is one prime reason explaining that identical messages may be subject to diverse interpretations by people receiving the message simultaneously.

In terms of communication in a negotiating situation, we are not faced with the decision of choosing between communicating and not communicating. Taciturnity can e.g. issue illuminating information to the other party. E.g. the answer you refuse to give in response to a police request can be highly illuminating from their point of view.

In the physical world a power, current or energy has to exist in order to trigger off an effect. This does not apply in the world of information and communication. The act of not submitting your tax return can have major consequences, or the missing gift to our parents on their golden wedding could provide them with meaningful information. I.e. nothing could be a cause in the field of information and communication, which is not the case in the physical world.

Situation framing

The purpose of a situation framing is here to be understood as establishing the value basis for the parities in addition to explaining the relevance of the situation to the parties.

Situation framing can to a great extent be compared to Goffman's (1959) idea that the critical factor is our understanding of our present situation and our expected behaviour in this situation. In the same way situation framing is also closely linked to problem definition and to Schutz's (1990) understanding of how actors in a situation define the social world.

Schutz and Goffman's point is that we present various aspects of ourselves to others. In other words it is only with a part of ourselves that we enter social contexts. Schutz underlines the importance of relevance in relation to the interests at stake in the situation at hand. It is relevance and the person's conviction which constitute the important elements when a person frames a situation. What Schutz wants to point out is the infinite number of social relations which can appear before the person, provided he does not frame it and decide on its status from his point of view. It is furthermore the importance we attach to our experiences which will constitute the frame for the situation into which we enter.

The point is that the social world we construct, is constructed on the basis of our experiences and available knowledge. This means that a social process is operational. I.e.: We do not receive impressions, signals, symbols, information etc. from the other party in a negotiation situation, and then interpret the impressions. It is just as much a process the other way round. We construct some notions and look for signs, signals, symbols, information etc., with which these notions are consonant in relation to the other party. In this way we manage to sustain our cognitive patterns and prejudices without new information budging our past experiences. Understood in this way the making of the social reality turns into an individual conservative process, and functions as a hindrance in our efforts to frame the negotiating situation in new ways.

Below follows the general model which will be discussed in the remainder of this chapter.

Figure 1 The proposed model for information in a negotiation context

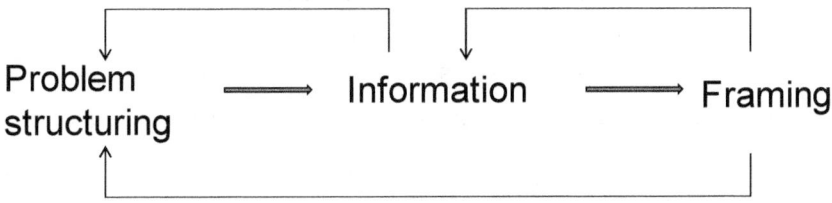

Problem definition

Boundaries of the negotiation issue

The boundaries of a phenomenon or a problem must always be drawn according to our purpose of the negotiations. Where we draw the boundaries is not a trivial matter. It is crucial to the outcome of our questions, even if exactly the same question about the same phenomenon or problem is asked. It is in other words the manner of defining a problem which provides the basis for the solution itself. At the same time it is fair to assume that our suppositions regarding the problem boundary will influence our various choices of action.

The fact that the parties draw the lines in different ways in connection with a negotiation problem, can be explained by means of three underlying mechanisms (Bandler and Grinder, 1975, Edelman, 1995; 1995a):

A. We generalise on the basis of reality.

B: We select in something and select out something else.

C. We make distortions and changes which we are not aware of.

It is fair to assume that the same processes are in operation when boundaries are drawn in connection with a negotiation problem, and are instrumental in the communication to others of a particular explanation or definition of a problem:

1. We generalise on the basis of our personal experiences.

2. To a great extent we choose selectively on the basis of our memory and

3. We distort or are creative in relation to what we select from our

memory, making

it distorted in relation to what we have stored initially.

Transferred to a negotiation situation this can be refereed to as "the fallacy of information", and leads to the following proposition.

Proposition 1: Interpretation of information in negotiations will be distorted on the basis of a need to sustain previous experiences, and may hinder or promote the win-win context to develop depending on these experiences.

Proposition 1 is linked to cognitive dissonance theory (Festinger, 1957; 1964), where the basic premise in theory is that individuals strive for consistency or consonance among her or his own cognition. In the practical situation it will be decisive to know the other parties experiences related to the situation under negotiation.

Context

Context is here understood as the psychological basis influencing our way of acting in the situation. Context must not be confused with the physical environment. It is psychological or, a mental framework determining our way of thinking and acting in various situations. Any context will be included in a larger context, which in turn will influence the previous one.

A phenomenon or a problem will hardly be understood equally, if the parties involved do not share notions as to which context applies. The context is only meaningful to us if we understand what its markers are.

One solution in negotiations has been described as integrating or win-win, when interests on the part of various parties are organised in a manner conducive to mutual benefits. Integrating solutions can be said to exist at a level above compromises. Compromises are simple solutions where differences in terms of distance between the parties (the negotiation zone) are divided.

How should we proceed in our attempts to change the negotiation situation, from a win-lose to a win-win situation? First, it is the problem having created the situation we must continuously focus on. This problem must be defined in such a way that it appears in a concrete way. When this is done, we thoroughly examine the attempted solutions, and document what these solutions have led to in relation to the problem. We find an analogy to the procedure with Wazlawick et al. (1974:110).

Proposition 2: The more concrete the boundaries of the problem are defined and previous resolution propositions are analysed and the more explicitly we have indicated the consequences of these resolution propositions, the greater is the probability of transforming the win-lose context into a win-win context.

If a negotiation is based on the mental premise that the only way of winning is that the other party loses, on many occasions both parties will lose.

One example of this is as follows: Two persons disagree on the division of an orange. They agree on dividing it in two equal parts. The one makes squeezed orange juice from his part, and disposes of the rest. The other squeezes out the juice and uses the remnants as ingredients for a cake. If the motives of both parties had been established in advance (or during the course of the process), they would both have benefited from a different model of division than the seemingly fair equal division. In order to create a win-win situation it is, among other things, important to establish the motives of the parties. To understand that usually mixed motives are involved in human interaction is fundamental both in relation to the analysis and structuring of a negotiation process, says Lax and Sebenius (1986:30).

Proposition 3: The more the motives of the parties are displayed, the greater the possibility that we can transform a win-lose context into a win-win context.

Motives can be divided into two categories (Schutz, 1990). One is the purpose we want to achieve. This is linked to future, goal, and result, which is a subjective category linked to the actor's awareness. The other main type is linked to the actor's background, psychological dispositions and the environment he has been influenced by. This is oriented towards the past and can be regarded as a more objective category where given entities are to be examined. The first type of motives can be established communicatively, whereas the latter can be clarified by means of historical investigations.

Systemic structuring

By systemic (Bunge, 1983a; 1985; 1985a) is here meant that the part and the complete structure must be viewed in context, but that the complete structure takes precedent over the parts. We are not talking about a cause relationship, but rather a relation, where the complete structure has a stronger impact on the parts than the parts have on the complete structure. The statement - the complete structure is more than the sum of the various constituents -, brings to mind a difference in terms of number or quantity between the components and the complete structure, as if were dealing with some magic of addition. It is not a question of adding up the parts, and then reaching the conclusion that by means of a magic formula, the entire structure should be more than the sum of components. What the statement refers to is critical differences or better qualitative differences. The systemic axiom can be expressed in the following way: The entirety is qualitatively different from the components.

In systemic thinking the main question is: Which pattern would constitute the links of a phenomenon or problem? It is in fact information, which provides us with access to understanding a pattern. Information which we receive and transmit over a period of time, constitutes contexts which disclose a pattern. It is information in these type of contexts which systemic structuring is referring to.

In order to obtain insight into a negotiation problem an important angle of incidence is, according to systemic thinking, to look at the relations that exist, and not the individual elements of the problem complex. This is also a central point with Weick (1979).

Normally we first analyse the individual problems in a problem complex, and then we look at how they are related. If we analyse the problem from the opposite angle of incidence, and try to find the relations first, this will more easily generate ideéas leading us to different and hopefully better results.

A systemic approach is an investigation of a pattern linking a phenomenon or a problem to form a complete integrated structure. It is the pattern in which the information is included which continuously should constitute our focus of attention, and not the individual elements in an event or action. The characteristic aspect of patterns is the difficulty to point out cause and effect. A pattern can metaphorically be regarded as a circle, and a circle has no beginning or end.

An important consequence of systemic structuring is the promotion of perspective insight between the parties. Perspective insight is "the ability to adopt the opponents' view point in structuring bargaining strategies", according to Neale and Bazerman (1983:380). They found that negotiators with a high level of perspective insight experience grater success, grant more concessions, and express greater understanding of other people's values and expectations, than negotiators with a small degree of perspective insight.

Proposition 4: Systemic structuring promotes perspective insight between the parties, and the greater the possibility that we can transform a win-lose context to a win-win context.

A technique to develop perspective insight is to leave it to the parties to place themselves in an imaginary future and imagine that the conflict or disagreement which would constitute the basis for the negotiations is resolved, and then look at how imagination managed to solve the conflict. This is a technique which Schutz (1990: 20, volume 1) and Weick (1979), among others, describe.

In order to understand the other party, we must reflect on the meaning attached to an experience or action by them (Luhman, 1992). Whitehead (1948) and Schutz (1990) say that the concrete facts appearing before us, are not as concrete as they may appear at the moment. To argue that facts as they enter our consciousness are concrete, Whitehead (1948:52) says, would be to make a concrete fallacy. A rhetorical subspecies of Whiteheads concrete fallacy to be observed in negotiation situations, is to use a supposed conclusion, commonly regarded as a reality, as one's basis, and then argue in favour of the necessity to implement certain measures to reach this very conclusion.

Information

Information exchange

An important part of a negotiation is oriented around exchange of information. We do however have a tendency to overestimate information supporting an attitude, supposition etc. which we already have, and underestimate information contrasting this attitude, supposition etc. We will rarely conduct an active search for information which would go against our existing ideas and attitudes. We find support for this contention with Pruitt & Carnevale (1993: 84) and Grzelak (1982). Our inclination to seek information which supports our established attitudes, instead of seeking information which can budge our attitudes is also an important point with

Watson (1960, 1968a; 1968b).

In a way we give priority to what we already know, and in this way we economise both in terms of information-seeking processes as well as information analysis, even if this on many occasions leads to systematic fallacies. The most provocative results regarding this phenomenon are probably to be found in the works of Tversky and Khaneman (1971; 1973; 1974; 1983).

Proposition 5: The greater the exchange of information between the parties, the greater the probability for a win-lose context being transformed to a win-win context.

The limitations of proposition 5 is that the information being exchanged must not be detrimental to the parties. Proposition 5 receives tentative support from Bazerman (1994), Thompson (1991), Zubek et. al. (1992), Fisher & Ury (1981), Lax & Sebenius (1986:31) and Raifa (1982:338).

Information analysis

The purpose of the analysis of information is to identify problem areas and elicit alternate possibilities. In information analysis we have the available and relevant information and know the goal. What we have to do here is to transform our knowledge to reach our goal.

While expectations say something about what a negotiation situation promises, experiences in a negotiation situation can be understood as the distinction between what was realised and what was possible in the actual situation. This distinction adds information value to the experiences, and thus influences the future selection of information.

The information analysis is meant to provide the negotiations with a focus, and is oriented towards a concrete result. In the information analysis a necessary (but not sufficient) condition is to know what we want to achieve. If we know what we want to achieve, why we want to achieve it, while knowing how this is going to be achieved, a strategic dimension has been added to the information analysis in a negotiation context.

If we are committed to a negotiation strategy, we will have a tendency to make positive evaluations of information supporting of this strategy, and ignore or underestimate information arguing against this strategy, according to Staw and Ross (1980).

It is important to realise that the basis constituted by a fixed strategy will greatly influence the perception of potential results. At a later time in the negotiation process, e.g. the original offer will be imminent as a reference framework. The basis is often the mooring around which the negotiations are drifting. Information is then gathered in relation to this basis. Quite a lot of research supports the hypothesis that the basis is critical for the final result (Bazerman and Neale, 1992:179).

It is the search patterns already established which will determine where further information is to be sought. E.g. we are inclined to seek information within the boundaries of an area where we already have good knowledge, and not areas where our information is deficient, i.e. availability precedes relevance.

Proposition 6: When we in negotiations have stipulated a target and realise that it cannot be reached, we still have a tendency to cling to the original target, which may hinder the transformation of a win-lose context to a win-win context.

Proposition 6 is counterintuitive and therefore requires further elaboration. The following comments contain some explanations and substantiate proposition 6:

We find it difficult to distinguish between previous decisions and future decisions related to the first one. This applies in particular to the presentation of negative signals regarding the previous decision (Northcraft and Wolfe, 1984).

We are inclined to evaluate positive information more positively than negative information regarding an original decision (Caldwell and O'Reilly, 1982).

We have a tendency to actively pursue positive information in support of the decision already made (Caldwell and O'Reilly, 1982).

We are inclined to transmit information to others which supports our original decision (Caldwell and O'Reilly, 1982).

We are inclined to selectively filter out information about others supporting our original decision (Caldwell and O'Reilly, 1982).

We are inclined to relay information to others which supports our original decision (Caldwell and O'Reilly, 1982)

We are inclined to wish to appear consistent (Staw and Ross, 1980).

We are inclined to reward managers who stay the course through positive feed-back, and are less supportive of managers who change the course (Ross and Staw, 1986).

We are led by psychological investments made in a project (Dawes, 1988: 22; Arkes and Blumer, 1985).

The goals are set higher and fewer concessions are gradually granted as the negotiator acquires more information (Thompson, 1990).

A long time perspective has according to a number of studies (Yukl, 1974; Smith et. al., 1982) been observed coincide with the maintenance of the original goal.

Choosing information type

Choosing information type is linked to the cognitive authority of information, i.e. why do we believe more in one type of information than another pertaining to the same problem area?

Information, according to Nisbet and Ross (1980:45-51), arouses and sustains our attention:

a) when it seems emotionally interesting

b) when it is concrete and provocative and

c) when it is close to us in time and space.

In a negotiation context emotional, concrete and imminent information can be critical for the outcome. It is fair to assume that a link between the three types of information will be more effective than if they are used separately. It is further fair to assume that the longer we are able to direct people's attention to the information we are presenting, and particularly the three mentioned information types, the more cognitive authority is attached to the information. This is in accordance with results form Tesser (1978), who explained this phenomenon as a result of a more activated memory.

It must further be emphasised that it is not only correct information which affects us in this manner. Erroneous information, linked to the emotional, the concrete, and the imminent is just as important, and we have difficulties in protecting ourselves against both the presentation of information and our own reactions to it in negotiations.

Proposition 7: The more effectively we manage to transmit correct information emotionally interesting, concrete, provocative and close to us in time and space, the greater is the probability of the information receiving high cognitive authority, and the greater the possibility that we can transform a win-lose context to a win-win context..

Proposition 7 indicated that information which is concretely, comprehensively and vividly described, affects us more strongly than information about the same event relayed in a more neutral fashion. If we through this verbal exposition manage to bring forth a picture in the other person's mind, this will reinforce a concrete and provocative piece of information. This can be accomplished by narrating anecdotes, stories and cases making the information transmitted more vivid, instead of providing more facts and statistical information. An example of this is the lobbying against Norwegian whaling. What the opponents of whaling have accomplished, is to portray a thinking, sensitive animal, tantamount to a prehistoric man swimming in his prehistoric sea in majestic isolation. By turning the whale into a human-like creature in people's minds, they have attained more public support than the proponents of whaling have through their statistical documentation of stocks and tolerance levels for taxation. To what avail is the documented tolerance of higher taxation levels, when in people's imagination the heart of the matter is the principal aspects of hunting for a human-like creature.

Framing

The value basis

To reach a thorough understanding of some other person's value basis is difficult. This is because parts of this basis is left out for various reasons when we introduce ourselves in the social situation. It might be exactly what we fail to communicate, which is the most powerful entity in the value system. Normally we express our value system some way or another, but it is probable that what we do not communicate which may constitute the most important information for the other party.

Furthermore it is the most basic values, also in a more subtle way, which are the ones which influence how we perceive the other party, and thus how we interpret his behaviour through our typologies. To acquire information about the other party's value system is thus instrumental in creating order in our view of the other party.

Instead of using the aims of the other person or his position in the negotiation process as our basis, a complementary angle of incidence could be to seek for values or norms inherent in a specific act performed by the person. By acquiring insight into the values behind individual acts, we can acquire information about the person's pattern of values, and thus be in a better position to understand his ostensible motives in the negotiation situation. The idea behind this angle of incidence is that people base their entire life philosophy on every-day actions and the understanding of those will in a certain limited context mean the ability to predicate future actions.

Through the entire process of socialisation, some mental variables are kept stable, while others are given various levels of leverage. It is fair to assume that variables which are kept stable, have a strong impact on the development of our value basis, while the variables which have greater leverage provide the opportunities for developing this value basis. A study of the value basis should with this supposition as a basic premise, start by looking at the mental variables in a system, which have been subject to stabilising efforts over some time. This will also give us knowledge about the other party in a negotiation situation.

A model for the analysis of the value basis is shown in figure 2.

Fig. 2 Analysis of the value basis

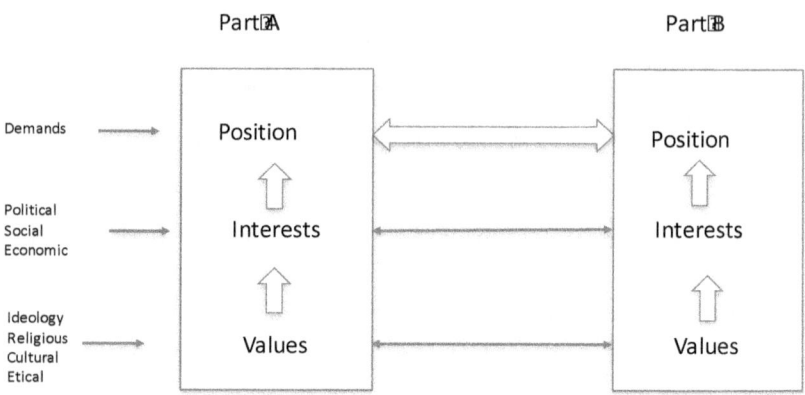

The model is based on the assumption that the value basis permeates the basic interests, and the position officially expressed in a negotiation situation. Position can be described as first order expression which we present to the other party. The basic interests can be said to be second order expression. These are more difficult to get access to, but determine the expressions of the first order. The value basis can be said to be the expression of the third order. These are rarely verbalised in a negotiation context, but if we manage to decode the third order expressions, we might find it easier to understand the expressions of the first and second order.

The model can be linked to the following questions:

What is the intended accomplishment, which is linked to position.

What is the purpose of achieving a result, which is linked to the basic interests.

What norms linked to the value basis are we trying to maintain.

Proposition 8: The more information we get about the value system of the other party, the greater is the probability that we can transform a win-lose context into a win-win context.

The value basis can be compared to the personal theories on the part of the actors, which can often be implicit and hidden for the person they are intended for, but with a strength level conducive to impacting all actions performed by the actors (see postulate 1). Lax and Sebenius (1986:215) say that interests constitute the measuring stick of negotiation. It may be true, but it is the value basis which constitutes these interests.

Relevance

Relevance in a negotiation context is closely linked to the development of positive emotions, because if we manage to develop positive emotions in a negotiation situation, it is fair to assume that the situation will be more relevant for the parties.

Emotions can be understood as the degree of involvement attached to a certain situation by us. There is no universally accepted definition of emotions, says Bowers et al. (1985:501 - 502). What we can do, however, is to look at what expression the emotions have. Anger, embarrassment, pride, joy and fear are all expressions of emotions.

How emotions affect a negotiation situation is one of the least studied areas in negotiation, according to Bazerman & Neale (1992: 123). This is further underlined by Pruitt & Carnevale (1993: 100) and Bowers et. al. (1985:500). One explanation of this might be that emotions are difficult to classify by the researcher and difficult to verbalise for those involved.

There are however some research results suggesting that positive emotions facilitate problem solving in negotiations. Baron (1990) and Baron et. al. (1990) have in their investigations documented this to a certain extent. The results from research on how emotions affect a negotiation situation suggest that positive emotions have the following effect:

Positive influence on having trust in others, and also improvements in terms of

final results (Kramer et al., 1990).

Improvement of the creative problem-solving faculty (Isen et. al., 1985).

A tendency to create win-win situations (Hollingshead and Carnevale, 1990).

An improvement of information exchange in negotiations (Carnevale and Isen,

1986).

Proposition 9: The more the parties succeed in developing positive emotions, the more information exchange between the parties will ensue, and the greater is the probability for developing a win-win context.

Positive emotions are associated with greater generosity and the readiness to help, in addition to their ability to solve problems creatively and alleviate aggression and reduce suspicion. Humour is, among other things, instrumental in toning down suspicion in a tense negotiation situation, according to Carnevale and Pegnetter (1985). The experience of justice is also conducive to the development of positive emotions (Withey & Cooper, 1989). Carnevale and Isen (1986) found in their study that positive emotions reduce aggressive tactics and increase the advantages (results) for both parties. Lewis and Fry (1977) found that this also happens when a physical barriers between the parties are removed.

We have a tendency to avoid risk linked to gaining profits, and run risks linked to escaping losses. To escape losses we have a tendency to display aggressive behaviour, while the behaviour is more defensive when it comes to gaining a profit. These are results for prospect theory research, reported by Kahneman and Tversky (1979) among others. A result of this theory is that the way a problem is limited or presented, can change the behaviour of the actors.

We can frame a situation as a win-lose or win-win context depending on to what point of reference we choose to use. E.g. if we are to sell a house or buy a new one, and make a decision in view of the valuation figure, the emotional experience of the sale will be quite different, than if we compare the monthly expenses of the house for sale with the identical expenses of the house we are purchasing. This is the reference point used by us in our estimates of whether something would mean losses or profits when we make up our minds whether to accept or reject and offer.

Prospect theory is an important breakthrough for the understanding of how important framing information is and how we make decisions in negotiation situations.

Proposition 10: The more we frame the problem, making it seem as if escaping losses is the main thing, the greater is the probability that aggressive behaviour is triggered, and the lower is the probability to transform a win-lose context into a win-win context..

Proposition 10 A: The more we frame the problem, making it seem as if profit is the ultimate goal, the grater is the probability that defensive behaviour is triggered, and the higher is the probability to transform a win-lose context into a win-win context..

Conclusion

If the theoretical statements in the chapter are correct, practical negotiation situations would benefit from having an analytical distinction between problem definition, information processes and situation framing, as:

1. Problem definition is crucial in relation to how we perceive the problem

2. Information processes are crucial in relation to what information we base our

   decisions on, and

3. Situation framing is crucial in relation to how we act in the situation.

The purpose of the chapter was to investigate under which conditions it could be expected that the negotiation parties substitute a competitive definition of the situation for a co-operative one. The main question we tried to answer in relation to this purpose was: How can we change a negotiation context from a win-lose situation to a win-win situation? Discussing ten propositions in relation to the purpose the following revised model of information management in negotiations could represent a tentative answer to the research question.

Fig. 3 The revised model of information in negotiation

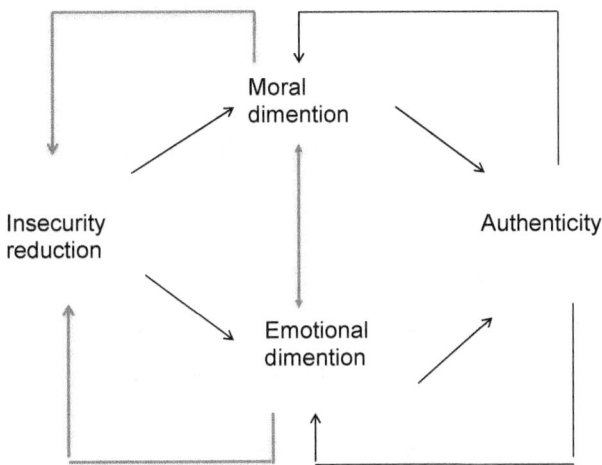

References

Arkes, H.R. & Blumer, C. (1985). The Psychology of sunk costs. Organizational Behavior and Human Performance, 35: 129-140.

Bandler, R. & Grinder, J. (1975). The Structure of Magia. Vol I og II, Science and Behavior Books, Palo Alto, Cal.

Baron, R.A. (1990). Environmentally induced positive affect: Its impact on self- efficacy, task performance, negotiation, and conflict. Journal of

Applied Social Psychology, 20: 368-384.

Baron, R.A., Fortin, S.P., Frei, R.L., Hauver, L.A. & Shack, M.L. (1990). Reducing organizational conflict: The role of socially induced positive affect. International Journal of Conflict Management, 1: 133-152.

Bateson, G. (1972). "Steps to an Ecology of Mind". Intex Books, London.

Bazerman, M.H. (1994). Judgement in Managerial Decision Making, John Wiley, New York.

Bazerman, M.H. & Lewicki, R.J. (red.) (1983). Negotiating in Organizations, Sage, New York.

Bazerman, M.H., & Neale, M.A. (1992). Negotiating Rationally, The Free Press, New York.

Bowers, J.W., S.M. Metts & W.T. Duncanson (1985). Emotion and interpersonal communication. I, M.L. Knapp & G.R. Miller, Handbook of Interpersonal communication (500-550), Sage, London.

Bunge, M. (1983). Exploring the World. Dordrecht: Reidel.

Bunge, M. (1983a). Understanding the World. Dordrecht: Reidel.

Bunge, M. (1985). Philosophy of Science and Technology. Part I. Dordrecht: Reidel.

Bunge, M. (1985a). Philosophy of Science and Technology. Part II. Dordrecht: Reidel.

Caldwell, D.F. & O´Reilly, C.A. (1982). Response to failures: The effects of choices and responsibility on impression management. Academy of management journal, 25: 121-136.

Carnevale, P.J. & Isen, A.M. (1986). The Influence of positive affect and visual access on the discovery of integrative solutions in bilateral negotiation. Organizational Behavior and Human Decision Processes, 37: 1-13.

Carnevale, P.J.D. & Pegnetter, R. (1985). The Selection of Mediation Tactics in Public Sector Disputes: A Contingency Analysis. Journal of Social Issues, 41: 65-85.

Cross, J.G. (1977). Negotiation as a Learning Process. Journal of Conflict Resolution, 21:581-606.

Dawes, R.M. (1988). Rational choice in an uncertain world, Harcourt Brace, New York.

Edelman, G.M. (1995). The Remembered Present: A Biological Theory of Consciousness, Basic Books, New York.

Edelman, G.M. (1995a). Bright Air, Brilliant Fire: On the Matter of the Mind, Basic Books, New York.

Festinger, L. (1957). A theory of cognitive dissonance. Stanford University Press, Stanford, CA.

Festinger, L. (1964). Conflict, decision and dissonance. Stanford University Press, Stanford, CA.

Fisher, R. & Ury, W. (1981). Getting to Yes: Negotiating Agreement without giving in. Houghton Miffin, New York.

Goffman, E. (1959). Presentation of Selv in Everyday Life, Anchor Books, New York.

Grzelak, J.L. (1982). Preferences and cognitive processes in interdependence situations: A theoretical analysis of cooperation. In V.J. Derlega & J. Grzelak (red.), Cooperation and helping behavior: Theories and research (95-122), Academic Press, New York.

Gulliver, P. (1979). Disputes and Negotiations: A Cross-Cultural Perspective, Academic Press, New York.

Hollingshead, A.B. & Carnevale, P.J. (1990). Positive affect and decision frame in integrative bargaining: A reversal of the frame effect. Best chapter Proceedings of the fifth Annual Conferance of the Academy of Management (385-389).

Isen, A.M., Johnson, M.M.S., Mertz, E. & Robinson, G. (1985). The Influence of positive affect on the unusualness of word associations. Journal of Personality and Social psychology, 48: 1413-1426.

Kahneman, D. & Tversky, A. (1979). Prospect Theory: An analysis of decision under risk. Econometrica, 47: 263-291.

Kochan, T. (1980). Collective bargaining and Organizational behavior. In, B. Staw and L Cummings (red.), Research in Organizational behavior, Vol. 2, JAI, Greenwich, CT.

Kramer, R.M., Newton, E. & Pommerenke, P. (1990). Selfenhancement biases in negotiations: Antecedents and consequences, Unpublished chapter, Dept of Organizational behavior, Stanford University, Stanford, California.

Lax, D.A. & J.K. Sebenius, (1986). The Manager as Negotiator, Free Press, London.

Lewis, S. & Fry, W. (1977). Effects of visual access and orientation on the discovery of integrative bargaining alternatives. Organizational Behavior and Human Performance, 20: 75-92.

Luhman, N. (1992). Ecological Communication. Polity Press, Cambridge.

Merton, R.K. (1949). Social Theory and Social Structure, Free Press, New York.

Miller, J.G. (1978). Living Systems. McGraw-Hill, New York.

Neale, M.A. & Bazerman, M.H. (1983). The role of perspectivetaking ability in negotiating under different forms of arbitration, Industrial and Labor Relations Review, 36: 378-388.

Nisbett, R.E. & Ross, L. (1980). Human inference: Strategies and shortcomings of social judgement, Prentice Hall, Englewood Cliffs, N.J.

Northcraft, G.B. & Wolfe, G. (1984). Dollars, sense and sunk costs: A life cycle model of resource allocation decisions. Academy of management Review, 9:225-234.

Polanyi, M. (1962). Knowledge and Being, Routledge, New York.

Pruitt, D.G. (1981). Negotiation behavior, Academica, New York.

Pruitt, D.G. (1991). Strategy in negotiation. I, Kremenyuk, V. (red.), International Negotiation: Analysis, Approaches, Issues, Jossey Bass, San Francisco.

Pruitt, D.G. & Carnevale, P.J. (1993). Negotiation in social conflict, Open University Press, Buckingham.

Putnam, L.L. (1985). Bargaining as Organizational Communication. I, R.D. McPhee & P.K. Tomkins (red.), Organizational Communication:

Traditional Themes and New Directions. Vol. 13, Sage, New York.

Putnam, L.L. (1985a). Bargaining as task and process: Multiple functions of interaction sequences. I, R.L. Street, jr. & J.N. Cappolla (red.), The social psychology of language: Sequence and pattern in communication behavior, Edward Arnold, London.

Putnam, L.L. & Poole, M.S. (1987). Conflict and negotiation. I, F.M.Jablin, L.L. Putnam, K.H. Roberts & L.W. Porter (red.),Handbook of Organizational Communication (549-599),Sage, London.

Raifa, H. (1982). The Art and Science of Negotiation. Harvard University Press, Cambridge, Mass.

Ross, J. & Staw, B.M. (1986). Expo 86: An escalation prototype. Administrative science quarterly, 31: 274-297.

Rubin, J.Z. & Brown, B.R. (1975). The social psychology of bargaining and negotiation, Academic Press, New York.

Schutz, A. (1990). The Problem of Social Reality, Collected Chapters, Vol. 1, 2 og 3, Kluwer Academic Publishers, London.

Smith, D.L., Pruitt, D.G., & Carnevale, P.J. (1982). Matching and Mismatching: The effect of own limit, others toughness and time pressure on concession rate in negotiation. Journal of Personality and Social Psychology, 42: 876-883.

Staw, B.M. & Ross, J. (1980). Commitment in an experimenting society: An experiment on the attribution of leadership from administrative scenarios. Journal of Applied Psychology, 65: 249-260.

Strauss, A. (1978). Negotiations: Varieties, Contexts, Processes, and Social

Order, Jossey Bass, San Francisco.

Tesser, A. (1978). Self-generated attitude change. I, L Berkowitz (red.), Advances in Experimental Social Psychology, Vol. 11, Academic Press, New York.

Thomas, W.I. (1928). The Child in America: Behavior Problems and Programs, New York.

Thompson, L.L. (1990). An examination of naive and experienced negotiators. Journal of Personality and Social Psychology, 59: 82-90.

Thompson, L.L. (1991). Information exchange in negotiation. Journal of experimental Social Psychology, 27: 161-179.

Tversky, A. & Kahneman, D. (1971). The belief in the law of numbers. Psychological Bulletin, 76: 105-110.

Tversky, A. & Kahneman, D. (1973). Availability: A heuristic for judging frequency and probability. Cognitive Psychology, 5: 207-232.

Tversky, A. & Kahneman, D. (1974). Judgement under uncertainty: Heuristics and biases. Science, 185: 1124-1131.

Tversky, A. & Kahneman, D. (1983). Extensional versus intuitive reasoning: The conjunction fallacy in probability judgment. Psychological Review, 90: 293-315.

Wason, P.C. (1960). On the failure to eliminate hypotheses in a conceptual task. Quarterly Journal of Experimental Psychology, 12: 129-140.

Wason, P.C. (1968). Reason about a rule. Quarterly Journal of Experimental Psychology, 20: 273-283.

Wason, P.C. (1968a). On the failure to eliminate hypothesis: A second look. I, P.C. Wason & P.N. Johnson Laird (red.), Thinking and Reasoning. Penguin, Harmandsworth.

Watzlawick, P., Bavelas, J.B. & Jackson, D.D. (1967). Pragmatics of Human Communication. W.W. Norton & Company, New York.

Watzlawick, P., Weakland, J. & Fish, R. (1974). Change, W.W. Norton & Company, London.

Weick, K.E. (1979). The Social Psychology of Organizing".2.nd. ed., Addison Wesley Publishing Company, London.

Whithead, A. (1948). Science and the Modern World, Mento Book, New York.

Withey, M. and Cooper, W.H. (1989). Predicting exit, voice, loyality and neglect. Administrative Science Quarterly, 34: 521-539.

Yukl, G.A. (1974). The effects of situational variables and opponent concessions on bargainers perception, aspiration, and concessions. Journal of Personality and social Psychology, 29: 237-236.

Zubek, J.M., Pruitt, D.G., Peirce, R.S., McGillicaddy, N.B. & Syna, H. (1992). Short term success in mediation: Its relationship to disputant and mediator behaviors and prior conditions. Journal of Conflict Resolution, 36: 546-572.

Chapter 2 Influence

Introduction

The objective of this chapter is to contribute to a perspective of information systems often neglected in information management literature, i.e. qualities of information and speaker causing more cognitive authority to be attached to one type of information than another. This phenomenon has a direct impact on management, as it has an effect on the information we exchange, how we interpret information, and how information is transformed into knowledge and used in making strategic decisions.

With information is here meant the difference in a message conducive to the perception of a difference relative to previous knowledge, or with Bateson (1972:272) "the difference which makes the difference".

With communication is here meant the exchange and sharing of messages between two or more parties. The connection between communication and information can be expressed by saying that the smallest unit in a communication unit is the information part. It is the contents of the latter which constitute the object of transmission to the other party. But the message also consists of a relationship part and a hierarchy part (Ruesch and Bateson, 1951). The relationship part says something about our relationship to the other(s) whom we are transmitting to, or receiving information from. The hierarchy part expresses the rank or level in terms of social standing or prestige on the part of the person sending or receiving information. In order to fully understand a message, it is therefore important to be conscious of all three components of the message, i.e. the relationship part, the hierarchy part and the information part.

With knowledge is here meant distinctions serving a purpose. With this definition of knowledge we also say that when distinctions operate on information, and systematise and structure this for a specific end, knowledge is developed. This definition is closely linked to Luhman's concept of knowledge (Luhman, 1986; 1992).

With information pragmatics we here mean the effects information has on the receiver (interpreter in fig. 1) and the sender (fig. 1).

By means of the previous definitions of information, information pragmatics, communication and knowledge, we have managed to link these entities in a coherent system. The chapter thus has relevance for knowledge building and knowledge integration in organisations, too. The definition of information and knowledge also links our contribution to Von Krogh, Roos and Slocum's (1994) work, even if the purpose of our contribution is of a more practical nature.

Lyles and Schwenk (1992), says that we have little knowledge of how knowledge structures actually develop. This chapter is a little contribution to fill this information gap.

The chapter is also linked to the development of the concept dominant logic, which Prahalad and Bettis (1986) developed and which has been further explained by Grant (1988); Ramanujan and Varadarajan (1989); Ginsberg (1990); Bettis and Prahalad (1995).

Bettis and Prahalad (1995:6-7, note 2) say: "What appears to be needed is not more data, but better frameworks in the sense of sufficient statistics that can facilitate interpretation". This chapter is a small contribution to develop a part of the framework for interpretation of data inquired about by Bettis and Prahalad.

The dominant logic is seen as "an information filter" (Bettis and Prahalad,1995:6). An important purpose in relation to dominant logic is here to provide a minor contribution to aspects of dominant logic in order to understand the strategy process on the basis of how and why one type of information has more cognitive authority than another. If we manage to make a contribution to this issue, we have shed light on aspects of dominant logic hitherto left in the dark. If, through the strategy process, greater knowledge of why one type of information has more cognitive authority than the other can be acquired, the ability on the part of the system to learn might be improved, as victimisation by dominant logic will cease.

As a result of increased knowledge about the process of filtering information, the ability on the part of organisations to develop organizational learning will be increased, as aspects of dominant logic will be uncovered and thus facilitate a less biased interpretation of data, and put the system in a better position to carry out information search procedures.

Believing in one type of information rather than another type of information, and making others believe in the information, is also linked to the act of influencing. The first person to ask questions about our inclination to believe more in one type of information than another seen from a social psychology perspective, was Lasswell (1948:37). He put it in the following way: Who says what, through which channels, to whom, and with what impact? If we break down that problem in several sub questions, the following elements will appear: The one who sends a message. The information itself. Media in operation. The recipient and interpreter of the message.

There are a number of available theories conducive to the acquisition of knowledge about this phenomenon. The first person to put an experimental focus on this phenomenon was Hovland (1953). The theories to be launched first were oriented towards three main variables: Attention towards information, comprehension of the information contents, degree of acceptance of the information conclusions. Later the processes behind the phenomenon has been extended. McGuire (1972) says that the following processes are important aspects of influencing: Presentation, awareness, comprehension of the information content, links to previous knowledge with the person and changes in the behaviour of the recipient. McGuire's argumentation is that no errors in the steps prior to behavioural changes must occur, if information is to bring about changes in behaviour on our part.

Most of the time people working in organisations generate and use information unreflectively, without regard to how, and why the information impacts ourselves and the environment. This will create problems, successes and threats in an ureflected way for the organisation. Strategies and plans may be created on the basis of this information, sometimes resulting in biases for those who are to operate the strategy. Strategies and plans may be modified as a result of action feedback. A more economical management of company resources would be to judge why we use some sort of information and knowledge developing the strategy, and how this affects the organisation and the environment.

Organisations are problem solvers, but they may create more problems for themselves using knowledge which is not judged for its pragmatics in beforehand.

Starbuck (1983: 91) says: "problem solving is defined by its origin, whereas decision making is defined by its ending-a decision". Maybe the opposite is true when it comes to strategic knowledge about information pragmatics, i.e. decisions about how to use and why to use information come before the problem solving phase. Maybe this is the paradox of why organisations seldom focus upon information pragmatics, but only information content.

It is the search for possible problems impacting managers when gathering and using information and creating knowledge which constitute the focus in this chapter, not problem solving.

It may not be irrelevant information or misinformation which is the greatest problem for managers gathering and using information, but rather the effect the relevant information has upon the managers and the receiver of this information. Relying on the companies information system may on some level equal relying on the management mis- information system, when information pragmatics is not reflected upon neither in the information system nor by the user of that system.

Using information without reflecting upon its pragmatics is irrational, i.e. the data may be correct, even the facts represented in the data may be correct, but the pragmatics of the data forming the basis for information may function as a bias in relation to the strategic decision. In this way correct facts about a problem or phenomenon may be used over and over again, but the strategy may not be rational or even "correct", because the information influences the decision maker and other actors in and outside the system in ways the strategy group is not conscious about; not because it is an unconscious process, but because the information pragmatics is not judged. In this way correct facts may become incorrect strategy.

People easily mix data with facts and facts with information, and information with knowledge, and they seldom ask why they are more inclined to believe in one type of information or knowledge rather than other types. But they certainly can answer why they believe in a fact. Using information seems to be a sort of spontaneous activity, whereas using facts is not.

People reacts quit differently to information, but there may be some general patterns of information which have an effect upon all of us. It is this general pattern we will try to uncover in this chapter.

We may filter information, but we cannot filter the pragmatics of information, we can only reflect upon it and react according to our reflections. It is the criteria which are fairly stable from situation to situation we try to uncover, not the variations information pragmatics has upon different people. We believe that reflecting upon these criteria may help managers be a little bit conscious about information pragmatics and not immune to its effects.

Perfect planning would imply perfect information, but if we had perfect information the planning would not be perfect, because the pragmatics of information is nearly never considered in the concept of perfect information. Perfect information as a concept is connected to what that information represent, not the pragmatics of the information itself. And if the pragmatics of information is not taken into consideration in the concept of perfect information (whatever that may be) perfect planning can not be reached even with perfect information.

The gathering and use of information in organisations is a sort of autopoietic system (Von Krogh et. al. 1994; Luhman, 1986, 1992), i.e. it reproduces the existing knowledge structures in the system, with little cognitive openness to the information effects upon the organisation. This is also the main message in the concept dominant logic, as we interpret it. This implies that little learning reaches the organisation, i.e. the organisation is bounded by its own pre-knowledge and norms. What is needed is knowledge about information pragmatics to open the system for learning. If a feedback-loop is designed between the information used and the information pragmatics learning may occur, i.e. the autopoietic system will open up in respect to information about information. If this consequence is taken into consideration we believe the strategic management process will be improved.

The organisations gather, process and use information, but it takes only responsibility for the semantics and content part of it, and not the pragmatic part, which may have a dementrial impact of the system as a whole. The strategy process itself will be affected by not making this distinction clear, and not taking responsibility for the pragmatics of information. Organisations cannot avoid using this distinction without affecting the effect of the strategy process itself. Information affects the internal state of the system, and the strategy is supposed to affect the environment. But if information pragmatics is not considered carefully the internal state as well as the strategic effect upon the environment may get out of control.

The organising idea behind the model (fig. 1) is that the cognitive authority of information is constituted by: an interpreter making use of certain cognitive processes and cognitive principles determining his information assessment, in addition to certain heuristic principles also in operation. The very message in communication is subject to certain information processes which are all of importance to a potential decision maker. Finally, characteristic features of the speaker or sender will impact the cognitive authority of the information.

We use the concept interpreter, and not receiver, as interpretations reefer to an active process, whereas receiver has connotations towards a more passive mode.

Figure 1. can be framed in the following way: The speaker, or the sender, has certain personal characteristic features which influence us. The message has certain properties which affect us. We, as interpreters of information, are instrumental in attaching certain characteristic features to the speaker as well as the information itself, which are not to be found with either.

Fig. 1 A general model of the cognitive authority of information

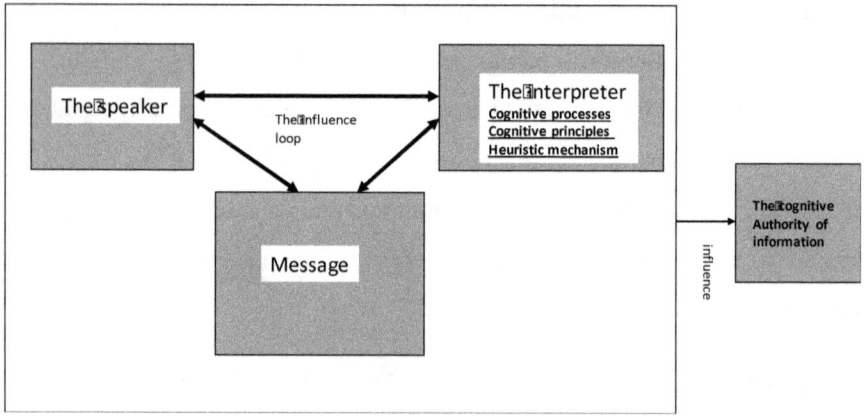

In the following section we discuss the abstract variables which constitute the main constructs in the model. Several propositions based on

the model are presented.

Interpreter

Cognitive processes

Two cognitive processes will henceforth be subject to discussion. These are expectation and typologies.

Expectation

Expectation can here be seen as an attributing process where certain boundaries with regards to possible outcomes are closely linked to a selection in a future situation.

Our expectations on behalf of a person will impact our reaction to his behaviour. If our impression of a person is that he should be trusted, our behaviour towards this person will reinforce this impression. If, on the other hand, another impression of this person has been created through rumours etc., our behaviour towards this person will be completely different. But it is even more serious. Our behaviour towards the person will reinforce the behaviour to be expected from this person. Rumours and prejudices in this way become mechanisms conducive to the realisation of the expected behaviour, and thus we in a sense get our notions "confirmed". This applies even if there is no element of truth in our expectations. The first person to report this phenomenon in human interaction was Kelly (1950). In this way expectations regarding other persons are intrinsically powerful, and rumours are more than just harmless information. Rumours and expectations are both instrumental in creating the person in the image preceding him through the rumour.

According to the expectation value model of Fischbein and Ajzen (1975), we are supposed to attach a certain expected subjective probability of occurrence to the object of reference. A reference object is the object to which the actual information is related. At the same time we attribute certain values to the object of reference, positive or negative. Our attitude to the reference object is then the sum of our expectations multiplied by the values attributed to it (attitude = the sum of expectations * value).

The point in this context is that it is fair to assume that information supporting our attitudes to the reference object will have more cognitive authority than information going against our attitudes. We will find support for this conclusion with Sheppard; Hartwich and Warshaw (1988).

Proposition 1: Information supporting our attitudes and notions has more cognitive authority than information going against our notions and attitudes.

The implications of strategy formation and dominant logic, provided that proposition 1 is correct, are that the flexibility of the system is greater if we actively seek information contrasting our attitudes and notions.

McGuire (1985) criticises the expectation value model, and states, among other things, that it may be guilty of considering only a few properties of the object of reference. But this does not affect the notion that there is a strong connection between one's attitudes and the cognitive authority on the part of information pertaining to the object of reference to us. What we do with this information is a different matter, i.e. to what extent it induces action on our part. In this context the topic of discussion is the cognitive authority of information, not how we act in relation to information, and then McGurie's criticism is only interesting insofar as it is capable of changing the attitude value itself, not the proposition as such.

One major point in the relation between one's attitudes to the object of reference and the confidence in information regarding this object, is that the two entities can vary interchangeably. The attitude may vary in different contexts and at different times, but the confidence in information pertaining to the object of reference may remain constant. E.g. for some reason we may have changed our attitudes to alcohol, in the way of reproaching alcohol. Our confidence in information expounding the harmful effects in terms of physical and social consequences, has then taken on a certain cognitive value for us. But in certain contexts and at certain times it is conceivable that we consume considerable quantities of alcohol. In these contexts our attitude too will be a different one, and probably more positive in terms of value. Our trust in information about the harmful effects of alcohol will still have the same cognitive value to us, also in situations when our attitudes to alcohol are changed.

Typologies

By typologies is here meant any expectation a perceiver has about how information may go together. Typology is aimed at guiding information processing and pre-processing, helping the receiver to fill in missing information and helping the receiver to quickly identify the appropriate information configuration (see Hastie, 1981).

What applies to expectations and rumours, has also the same status in terms of previous knowledge about a person. We have an inclination not to let the person expose himself in the situation. We make use of previous experience about similar types, and then we make our judgement on the person in question on the basis of our own typologization. In other words, it is other persons, with whom we have had some kind of experience at some time, who determine how we are going to behave towards a person we know nothing about. Once a person has entered our typology files, he is captured in an information enclosure, in which dominant logic operates. The result will be that typologization creates a person in the image we have in our typology file. If the person behaves contrary to our typologies, our reaction will be unease, uncertainty, and a negative behaviour towards the person will ensue, according to Garfinkel (1967:42 - 44.)

Proposition 2: Information supporting our typologies has more cognitive authority than information which does not support our typologies.

The consequences for the development of strategies and dominant logic is that communicatively we have increased our awareness of typologies in our possession. Otherwise our evaluations of other people and information presented by them might easily be biased.

Once we have formed an opinion about a person through our typologies, we are inclined to overlook information contrasting this opinion, and will deliberately look for information supporting our established typology files. Information closure having genuine authority over most of us, is the statement level in proposition 2.

Cognitive principles

Principles to be discussed in the following presentation are: the contrast principle, the mutuality principle, the consistency principle, the publicity principle, the charisma principle, the authority principle, the scarcity principle and the principle of cognitive reflex. We will briefly make a survey of these principles insofar as they are relevant for the cognitive authority of information, and dominant logic.

The contrast principle:

If a piece of information which alone would have a negative effect, follows a piece of information which is not suitable for us, we have a tendency to overestimate the last piece of information. This principle can be used in many contexts to make one piece of information presented after another look better than would have been the case if presented first or alone (see Kenrick et. al., 1989; Kenrick and Guitierres, 1980).

Proposition 3: If we present negatively slanted information irrelevant to the actual situation prior to negatively slanted information relevant to the actual situation, the negative relevant information will be inclined to instil a sense of relief in the receiver and thus have more impact than if presented alone.

Consequences for the strategy process and dominant logic are that information which depends on a lot of effort to have an impact, must be combined with information pointing in the direction of a worst case scenario, and this must appear prior to relevant information.

The mutuality principle:

If we receive something before having to give away something, we are more likely to give back. This principle is in literature often referred to as information without cost (see Kunz and Wolcott, 1976; Riley and Eckenrode, 1986).

Proposition 4: If we receive information free of charge, which would normally not have been, or been inaccessible, we are more inclined to give information which would normally have been reserved for the person supplying us with information in the first place.

Benchmarking can to a great extent be viewed as being built on this principle. Companies make information about their processes, functions etc. available for national and international bench- marking partners, and receive information back which would have come with great difficult and at a considerably higher price than is now the case.

The consistency principle

Once we have made a choice, or taken a stand, we will experience personal mental pressure, and also pressure from the environment in the direction of behaviour consistent with the choice or position we have taken. This has, among other things, been reported by Rosenfeld, Kennedy and Gacalone (1986).

The explanation on the part of social psychology to the consistency principle, is obligation, i.e.: If we are to oblige someone to take a loose position, we will tie them up in the consistency principle.

Proposition 5: If we can make someone vaguely and suggestively make a commitment by giving information, this will next induce the person to give information which otherwise would have been withheld.

The consistency principle has in social psychology been developed as a theory by Festinger (1957). The basic premise in this theory about cognitive dissonance is that individuals strive for consistency in cognition. What proposition 5 expresses is that this also applies too information.

Several techniques are used to obligate people, e.g. to start slowly and build on the previous obligation. To make people say "maybe" in a an interview, may be the first step in an entire research chain relative to a problem area. For the person being asked, this implies: If you do not feel like being interviewed, do not commit yourself to the more trivial requests.

Another technique is to make the person write down some of his requests himself, or make a non-binding agreement. We tend to live up to what we write ourselves to a greater extent than what others do, even if it is by no means more legally binding.

A third technique is to make the persons expose their views to others. As soon as this is done, the person will have a tendency to have more consistency between his actions and/or standpoint.

A fourth technique is to make persons feel that the proposal really came from themselves, while in reality it was somebody else's original proposal.

The relevance of the strategy process and dominant logic can be to establish contact with people potentially adverse to the strategy at an early stage, and thus obligate them through the consistency principle.

The consistency principle can however lead to a situation where the issue behind the decision is not subject to critical scrutiny, i.e. the action sequence can easily become automatic.

The publicity principle:

This principle expresses that we perceive something as correct, because other people deem it correct. If we succeed in expressing the fact that it is a public truth we present, the other party will be inclined to agree to "this public truth".

Proposition 6: Information brought forth as a publicly accepted truth has high cognitive authority.

The publicity principle has the strongest effect on people who have low self-confidence, find themselves in an ambiguous situation, or are overcome by uncertainty. The reason for this statement and for proposition 6 is found in social impact theory, among other things (see Latane, 1981; Tanford and Penrod, 1983).

In the strategy process and for dominant logic, the critical element in reducing the impact of this special effect, is for special information Contrapreneurs to take on the task of pointing out the social impact of the information cognitive authority to people with a high status or rank in circles emulated and admired by the company. Otherwise, the ensuing strategy might easily turn into what the main stream follows, and competitive edges will be easily lost when all use the same information source.

The charisma principle:

Persons of great physical attraction to us tend to generate more agreement on our part, than people who are less physically attractive (see Benson et. al., 1976). These people will thus get an edge also in terms of relaying information to others, even if their knowledge within the actual field is not particularly deep. This principle also applies to qualities beyond physical ones; talent, friendliness, honesty and intelligence (see Eagley et al., 1990). By possessing, or appearing to posses, some of these qualities, these persons will find it easier to influence others by their views and to change our attitudes.

Proposition 7: Information stemming from persons with physical charisma and who are held in high esteem by their peers, has great cognitive authority.

Another factor supporting this principle is knowledge and contact with the persons in question. In the extension of this principle it also follows that if we can make the largest possible number of people identify with the thing or person to which/whom the information is related, it might be easier to pave the way for the message. To establish a strategy which will be met by a certain amount of opposition within the company, this principle can prove fruitful.

The authority principle

Requirements from authorities have a direct impact on why one type of information has a stronger impact than other types of information. The Milgram studies (1974) indicated this quite clearly. Briefly Milgram's studies explained that persons used for experiments inflicted on other persons what the persons used for the experiments took to be physical pain inflicted on the other person. In most cases the results of these studies implied that the persons used for the experiment by means of pressure from imminent authorities would put the other person through what they mistook for physical pain. In reality no pain was inflicted on the other person by the persons used for the experiment.

Milgram's explanation is that pressure from authorities exists in a systematic process of socialisation in our society.

Proposition 8: Information endorsed by people with a high social status and prestige in our society has high cognitive authority.

Authority symbols further have a certain authority on our thinking. Some research has indicated that titles (see Peters and Ceci, 1982; Ross, 1971), clothes (see Bickman, 1974; Bushman, 1988), and objects generating an aura of status and position (see Dodd and Gross, 1968) have a strong impact on our faith in persons who legitimise themselves through these symbols of authority.

For the strategy process and dominant logic it becomes important to reflect on the contents of this principle, as automatic interpretation processes might easily occur.

The scarcity principle

The principle expresses the following idea: Various entities appear to be more valuable to us if they are less accessible. Tversky and Kahneman (1983) express this principle as people's inclination to be more motivated by the fear of losing something than the thought of achieving something at the same price.

Scarce objects are also perceived as qualitatively better than objects readily available (Lynn, 1989).

Limitations imposed on our freedom, and particularly the freedom we have managed to achieve, tend to be targets of fierce reaction. The psychological Reactance theory, developed by Brehm (1966) and further developed by Brehm and Brehm (1981), provides an extensive explanation of people's reaction to the loss of personal freedom, and why we react so strongly to what we experience as a limitation imposed on our freedom.

Proposition 9: Information which is somehow "classified" and then made available, has high cognitive authority.

If limitations are imposed on our access to information, it is fair to assume that our reaction will be similar to our other restrictions on various types of freedom achieved. We will want more of this type of information, and we are inclined to believe more firmly in it, even if we are deprived of access to it. This has been described by Warchel (1992), among others.

A strategy to make people request and believe more in one type of information, could be to have it censored one way or the other, e.g. withheld from the public, and then make it publicly known that it as been subject to limited access. The same thing happens if public institutions elect to withhold information from public view. We are then inclined to regard this as more valuable information. And should something seep out behind closed doors, the verity of this information tends to be subject to less critical judgement, than if it was presented to us instantly. This could be one explanation why rumours and gossip have such proven impact.

For the strategy process and the dominant logic it is important to be aware of this phenomenon, as the acquisition of information in the strategy process can easily be biased if others are making conscious use of this principle.

The principle of cognitive reflex

It is very difficult to disprove a line of thinking where the chain of argument is logically consistent, but where the conclusion is not in accordance with the premises of argumentation. In the same way erroneous statements can be created on the basis of a logically sound and coherent chain of argument, because of an erroneous basis for premises. We use the expression **because** consciously in the preceding sentence, as it has turned out that this expression elicits a positive response to a wish irrespective of whether what follows the because sentence gives any explanatory or elaborate information or not.

Proposition 10: Information which contains because sentences has great cognitive authority.

Several studies done by Langer, Blank and Chanowitz (1978) and Langer (1989), among others, substantiate proposition 10. One example shown by Langer is the following: In a line in front of a Xerox machine, a student utters: Excuse me, can you please let me pass the line, because I have a lecture to catch. This generated 94% positive responses in several tries. When the because sentence was omitted, the rate of positive responses was 64%. When the because sentence provided no sensible additional information like e.g.: Excuse me, can you please let me pass the line, because I have to copy, there were 93% positive responses. Intuitively, this appears to be wrong. The explanation is that the word **because** appears to elicit an automatically positive reflex in most of us. It is arguably a cognitive reflex, where the message linked to the explanatory category (here: **because**) has more cognitive impact than a message not linked to an explanation category. An explanation to this cognitive authority of information can be our socialisation into the linear causal thought patterns, where the word **because** elicits the cause component in a linear-causal chain (see Fiske and Taylor, 1984: 58-60).

In the presentation of a strategy this principle will be crucial, particularly if what follows the sentence is linked to the aforementioned principles in this part of the chapter.

Heuristic mechanisms

In our evaluation of what information is most suitable in a situation, we often use heuristic evaluation mechanisms. The problematic aspect of heuristic evaluation mechanisms is that we are not conscious that we use them, according to Bazerman (1994:47). The heuristically mechanisms can further lead to systematic errors in our evaluations.

There are four heuristic evaluation mechanism often used on an everyday basis. These are:

We use information available at the moment (information at hand).

We use what is most distinctive in memory.

We use an initial mooring point as our basis

We make comparisons with similar cases.

Information at hand

We have a tendency to use information available at the moment, and ignore critical basic information. Critical basic information appears to be used when no information seems to be available, Kahneman and Tversky report (1972; 1973). It can appear as if the most conspicuous information is given most emphasis and most frequently used (see Alba and Marmorstein, 1987).

Proposition 11: Information available in a situation (information at hand), e.g. rumours have great cognitive authority.

A possible explanation can be that a survey of critical basic information is time-consuming and requires "boring" procedures with collection of basic data, among other things. In the strategy formation process and for the dominant logic it is critical to be conscious of this mechanism, as critical basic information can easily be lost if we not reflect on the consequences of using information at hand.

We use what is most prominent in memory.

We have a tendency to emphasise information which is easily retrieved from memory, according to Tversky and Kahneman (1973;1983).

As a rule we are not so good at recalling how an uncertain situation was perceived by us prior to the available results of our decision. I.e. we have a tendency to let the results influence strongly what we originally believed, prior to the results. This has been documented by Fishhoff (1975; 1975a; 1977).

Proposition 12: Information which is easily retrievable from memory has great cognitive authority.

Fishhoff's interpretation results unambiguously point to the fact that results increase the belief, on the part of individuals, that it is exactly these results they would have predicted, even if they did not have access to the results. One explanation of this phenomenon is that from a purely cognitive perspective, result knowledge is prominent in memory, and thus instrumental in guiding our presumptions regarding our opinions prior to an event. In a strategic context, and for dominant logic the link between processes constituting proposition 11, and proposition 12, could be very detrimental to the end results of this process, because information criticism and information quality can easily bias the outcome of the strategy process.

Initial mooring point

The size of a selection is fundamental in statistics, but the size of the selection does not seem to be an essential part of our intuitive understanding, according to Tversky and Kahneman (1971; 1974); Dawes (1988), among others. The extreme case is of course when we generalise from a few single incidents, and pass it off as a general truth.

We seem to be frozen in our own experiences based on a small selection. "I have personal experience", seems to have more impact, than a submitted research finding flawlessly executed.

Proposition 13: Information to which we have a personal relation in terms of experience, even if the basis for experience is scanty, has great cognitive authority.

Studies by Slovic and Lichtenstein (1971), among others, have indicated that we are easily caught up in perceptibly irrelevant information, and use this as basis for further evaluation. In most cases the final decisions are systematically drawn towards the initial information presented to us, according to Tversky and Kahneman (1973). Unfortunately, it is so that when people's knowledge about a field decreases, their confidence in their personal sense of judgement does not decrease accordingly (see Pitz, 1974).

In the strategy process and for the dominant logic it will be of critical importance to make this element an object for reflection, as final decisions could be biased by this phenomenon.

We make comparisons with similar cases

We have a tendency to evaluate all information in the light of previous results, and expect these results to continue to apply. This has been indicated by Kahneman and Tversky (1973), among others. We also have a nasty habit of overestimating correlated events (see Bar-Hillel, 1973), and underestimating events which occur independently of each other (see Tversky and Kahneman, 1974).

Proposition 14: Information linking two or more events has more cognitive authority than information which does not link the events.

When two events are linked the presumed probability of their occurrence is greater than if the events were not linked. Two examples from Tversky and Kahneman (1983) shed light on proposition 14.

Example 1:

In an investigative study it was found that experts presumed (asked in 1982) it to be less probable that:

1. Diplomatic relations between the USA and the Soviet Union would be broken in 1993, than that

2. A Soviet invasion of Poland would sever diplomatic ties between the USA and the Soviet Union.

NB: It would be conceivable that the Soviet Union could invade other countries than the Soviet Union, and thus effectively break off diplomatic relations, and this implies that 1 is more probable than 2, even if 2 turned out to have more cognitive authority.

Example 2:

a) A great tidal wave afflicting North America sometime in 1989 killing 1000 people, was estimated to be less probable than

b) an earthquake in California, eliciting a flood wave, effecting the death of 1000 people.

Elementary reflection should imply that there is a greater probability for a) to occur than b), since b) is a component in a), and many other events could lead to a.

A reflection of this phenomenon ought to reinforce the quality of the strategy process and create greater understanding of aspects pertaining to the dominant logic, as the results of this process could easily be biased if the phenomenon is not clarified for the parties involved.

Message

We have chosen to include all information processes in this part of the chapter, even if it might have been even more correct to discuss information sharing and information analysis under cognitive processes. It is more a structural issue than an analytical distinction which explains this choice.

Information processes

The purpose of information processes in strategic management is here regarded as:

* information sharing (exchange of information)

* analysis of information, making it suitable for our quest for the desired result,

* choosing type of information.

The basis for the selection of these information processes are to be found in Miller's (1978) theory. Another common way of categorising information processes used by social cognition theory (see Fiske and Taylor, 1984; Markus and Zajonic, 1985; Stephan, 1984) is to divide information processing into: Encoding, representation and retrieval. Nevertheless for the analytical purpose of this chapter we shall use the division listed first.

Information exchange (information sharing)

An important part of the strategy process is centred around exchange of information. We have, however, a tendency to overestimate the value of information supporting an attitude, notion etc. which we already have, and to underestimate information not supporting these attitudes, suppositions etc. We find support for this conclusion with Pruitt and Carnevale (1993:84); Grzelak (1982). The fact that we are inclined to look for information supporting our notions and convictions is also a major point with Wason (1960; 1968; 1968a).

Proposition 15: Information clashing with our previously established attitudes, suppositions and notions, has little cognitive authority.

In a way we give priority to what we already know, and in this way we also economise with both information-seeking processes and information analysis, even if this on many occasions leads to systematic erroneous inferences. The most provocative findings with regards to this phenomenon may be found in the works of Tversky and Kahneman (1971; 1973; 1974; 1983). Proposition 15 is partly substantiated by Bazerman (1994); Thompson (1991); Zubek et. al. (1992); Fisher; Ury and Patton (1991); Lax and Sebeenius (1986: 31); Raifa (1982: 338).

For the strategy process and the dominant logic, deliberate and active pursuit of information contrasting the dominant notions, might bring about more flexibility for the system.

Information analysis

In information analysis we have the information which is available, in addition to relevant information, and we know the goal. What we have to do here is transform what we know in order to reach the goal. If we have made a commitment to a strategy, we will have a tendency to make a positive evaluation of information supporting this strategy (see Stew and Ross, 1980). It is important to realise that the basic position, which corresponds to a fixed strategy, influences the perception of possible results strongly. A great deal of research supports the hypothesis that the basic position is critical for the final outcome (see Bazerman and Neale, 1992:179).

It is the seeking patterns already established which will decide where to pursue further information. E.g. We have a tendency to seek information within the areas where we already have plenty of knowledge, and not in the areas where our knowledge is deficient, i.e. it may seem like availability precedes relevancy.

Proposition 16: When we in the strategy process have set a goal for ourselves and we see that the goal cannot be reached, we have a tendency to still cling to the original goal, i.e. information supporting an established goal has great cognitive authority.

Proposition 16 is contra intuitive and therefore needs further elaboration. Here are some explanations supporting proposition 16:

*We have difficulties in distinguishing between earlier decisions and future decisions related to the former. This is particularly the case when negative signals about the previous decision are presented (see Northcraft and Wolfe, 1984).

*We have a tendency to actively seek positive information in support of a decision already made by us (See Caldwell and O'Reilly, 1982).

*We have a tendency selectively to filter out information which does not support an initial decision (see Caldwell and O'Reilly, 1982).

*We have a tendency to relay information supporting our decision to other people

(see Caldwell and O'Reilly, 1982).

*We have an inclination to try to appear as consistent (Staw and Ross, 1980).

*We have a tendency to reward leaders on a steady course with positive feedback, and to a lesser extent leaders who are inclined to do the opposite (see Ross and Straw, 1986).

*We are controlled by psychological investments laid down in a project (see Dawe, 1988:22; Arkes and Blumer, 1985).

*A long time perspective in several studies (see Yukl, 1974; Smith et. al., 1982) is found to correspond to sustaining the original goal.

For the strategy process and the dominant logic, clarification of this phenomenon will be of major importance, as automatic processes appear to pull in the direction of continuing a strategy not necessarily suitable for the system.

The choice of information type

Information, according to Nisbet and Ross (1980:45 - 51) weakens and sustains our attention:

a) when it appears to be emotionally interesting

b) when it is concrete and provocative and

c) When it is close to us in time and space.

It is fair to assume that a link between the three types of information will generate a stronger effect than separate use. It is further likely that the longer we manage to direct people's attention towards the information we present, and particularly the three former types of information, the greater cognitive authority can be attributed to the information. This is in accordance with results from Tesser (1978), who explained this phenomenon by pointing to the ensuing activation of or memory.

It should further be underlined that not only correct information has this effect on us. Misinformation, linked to the emotional, the concrete and the immediate, appears to have equal importance, and we have difficulties in protecting ourselves against both the information presentation and our own reactions to it.

Proposition 17: Information which creates concrete mental images have great cognitive authority.

One example of this phenomenon is the argumentation against Norwegian whaling. What the opponents of whaling have managed is to create a picture of a thinking, sensitive animal, quite similar to a prehistoric man swimming in a prehistoric ocean in majestic solitude. By turning the whale into a human-like being in people's minds, they have been able to achieve greater results opinion wise than proponents of whaling with their statistics on the tolerance level of natural stocks being consistent with the level of taxation. To what help is it that the stocks have a tolerance level compatible with the actual hunting, when in peoples minds an image of hunting for a human-like being has been conjured up?

The speaker

Characteristic features of the speaker

The appearance

Why do we have more faith in one person than another? Does appearance and how we appear before others mean anything for their confidence in information presented by us?

Several studies report that our confidence in other people's information is determined by their outer appearance. Examples of such studies include Dermer and Thiel (1975); Dion et. al. (1972); Rucker et. al. (1981); Hatfield and Srecter (1986); Ross and Salvia (1975). It should however be underlined that the results are not wholly unambiguous. We are also negatively prejudiced towards people with an attractive outer appearance. This applies both to men and women (see Kleinke and Staneski, 1980; Hatfield and Sprecher, 1986).

The courtroom is an example of a situation where credibility is definitely at stake. Even here, where law and justice should take centre stage, it appears that, according to substantial research, how a person looks, dresses, or otherwise appears has major impact on the outcome of the case. This has been thoroughly documented by Hatfield and Sprecher (1986) etc.

An important point is naturally not only how the other person appears before us, but how we feel that we appear in relation to others. Self-realisation and status impact each other reciprocally. Self-realisation here denotes how we experience our relationship with others. Status is to a certain extent a by-product of self-realisation. Quite often self-realisation and status will constitute our basis for evaluation.

Proposition 18: If a person signals that he is above or below a supposed average relative to peers in a certain situation, the person's information will have less cognitive authority than if he signals that he is on an average level in relation to his peers.

This may seem as a paradox (and contradict proposition 8). On the one hand we have confidence in people who are themselves, but when they are themselves, we do not have complete confidence in them.

For the presentation of the strategy, insight into this phenomenon can be used to give our own views more impact.

Competence and the ability to create confidence

Wilson (1983:13) underlines that the cognitive authority on the part of information is linked to a relationship between two persons, and that there will always be various degrees in terms of this authority. He further points out that the cognitive authority is linked to areas of interest. With the Information Cognitive Authority (ICA), he means exactly the question linked to why we are inclined to believe more in one type of information than another.

If we look at Information Cognitive Authority (ICA) linked to competence and confidence, the model in figure 2 can illustrate the relation. We find some support for the model with Wilson (1983).

Figure 2 Confidence and competence

The other persons competence		Little	high
	high	Information has little cognitive authority	Information has high cognitive authority
	Little	Information has little cognitive authority	Information has medium cognitive authority
		Little	high

Our trust in the person

This model indicates that if we have little confidence in a person, but the person has great competence in the area in focus, the person's information will only have medium cognitive authority in relation to us.

If, on the contrary, we have great confidence in the person, and he has great competence within the particular field, the person's information will have great cognitive authority in relation to us.

If we have little confidence in the person and his competence within the field is limited, the persons information will have little cognitive authority in relation to us. If, on the contrary, we have great confidence in the person, and his competence within the field is limited the model presupposes that the person's information has medium cognitive authority in relation to us.

Proposition 19: Competence within a given area, and our confidence in the person are positively correlated to information cognitive authority

For the strategy process and the dominant logic reflection around this phenomenon could boost the performance and the influence of the strategy.

Conclusion

Practical implications

The realisation of why we are more easily influenced by one type of information and one type of person than another type of information and another type of person, could put us in a position to shield ourselves from this influence in a strategy process, and also have a positive impact on reflection around dominant logic. This knowledge can be a further help if we want to influence others in the same strategy process ourselves.

Knowledge of how information influences participants in a strategy process, and how they deliberately or accidentally influence other by their information and manner, could have a major effect on the outcome of the strategy process. There is a clear connection between the cognitive value of information and our application of this information. If we do make no reflections on this context, systematic erroneous inferences could occur, detrimental both to the company and the surroundings.

A general methodology linked to figure 1, and the discussion around this model in this chapter in order to increase the competence in a strategy process to this aspect of the process, in addition to bringing to light aspects of the dominant logic, are the following:

1. Gathering information in a strategy process.

*Discuss information cognitive authority (ICA) linked to cognitive processes and reflect on proposition 1 and 2.

*Discuss ICA linked to cognitive principles and reflect on proposition 3-10.

*Discuss ICA linked to heuristic mechanisms and reflect on proposition 11-14.

*Discuss ICA linked to information exchange and reflect on propositions 15

*Discuss ICA linked to characteristics of source and reflect on propositions 18 and 19.

2. Processing of information in a strategy process

*Discuss ICA linked to information analysis and reflect on proposition 17.

A structured methodology of this kind could put the actors in the strategy process in a position to both prevent the unconscious use of information capable of infusing or hindering the strategy process, and consciously utilise knowledge to influence others in the intended direction.

Theoretical implications

If we define a theory as a system of propositions (Bunga, 1983:324), a variable analysis of the individual propositions will provide links between propositions, thus tying them together in one coherent system. The system of propositions which P1 - P19 constitute can be a starting point for systematic hypothesis generation and a testing of those hypotheses.

The interpretation pattern which controls the dominant logic determines the outcome of:

1. What type of information we initially gather in a strategy process.

2. How we generalise from reality

3. How we change and distort the information content put before us.

The dominant logic in this way runs strategic choices made by the system. A cognitive opening of the information filter might generate a development of a knowledge process in the activity, instigating the use of several interpretation models, inducing greater variation in terms of perspective, and expanding the action repertoire for the system. It is, however, the interaction between the dominant logic and the cognitive opening of the information filter which can put the system in a position to increase the quality of the strategy process, as putting emphasis on the cognitive opening of the information filter, exclusively, will lead to an overblown interpretation scope, while exclusive emphasis on the dominant logic will cut down the interpretation scope too radically.

References

Alba, J.W. and H. Marmorstein (1987). The effects of frequentcy knowledge on consumer decision making, Journal of Consumer Research, 14: 14-25.

Arkes, H.R. and C. Blumer (1985). The Psychology of sunk costs, Organizational Behavior and Human Performance, 35: 129-140.

Bar-Hillel, M. (1973). On the subjective probability of compound events, Organizational Bahavior and Human Performance, 9: 396-406.

Bateson,G. (1972). Steps to an Ecology of Mind. Intex Books, London.

Bazerman, M.H. (1994). Judgement in Managerial Decision Making. John Wiley, New York.

Bazerman, M.H. and M.A. Neale (1992). Negotiating Rationally. The Free Press, New York.

Benson, P.L., S.A. Karabenic and R.M. Lerner (1976). Pretty pleases: The effects of physical attractiveness on race, sex and receiving help, Journal of Experimental Social Psychology, 12: 409-415.

Bettis, R.A. and C.K. Prahalad (1995). The Dominant Logic: Retrospective and Extension, Strategic Management Journal 16 (1) pp. 5-14.

Bickman, L. (1974). The social power of a uniform, Journal of Applied

Social Psychology, 4: 47-61.

Brehm, J.W. (1966). A Theory of Psychological Reactance. Academic Press, New York.

Brehm, S.S. and J.W. Brehm (1981). Psychological Reactance, Academic Press, New York.

Bunge, M. (1983). Exploring the World. Dordrecht: Reidel.

Bushman, B.J. (1988). The effects of apparel and compliance, Personality and Social Psychology Bulletin, 14: 459-467.

Caldwell, D.F. and C.A. O'Reilly (1982). Response to failures: The effects of choices and responsibility on impression management, Academy of management journal, 25: 121-136.

Dawes, R.M. (1988). Rational choice in an uncertain world. Harcourt Brace, New York.

Dermer, M. and D.L. Thiel (1975). When beauty may fail, Journal of Personality and Social Psychology, 31: 1168-1176.

Dion, K., E. Berscheid and E. Hatfield (1972). What is beautiful is good, Journal of Personality and Social Psychology, 24: 285-290.

Doob, A.N. and A.E. Gross (1968). Status of frustrator as an inhibitor of hornhonking response, Journal of Social Psychology, 76: 213-218.

Eagly, A.H., R.D. Ashmore, M.G. Makhijan and L.C. Longo (1990). What is beatiful is good, but-: A meta analytic review of research on the physical attractiveness stereotype, Psychological Bulletin, 110: 101-121.

Festinger, L. (1957). A theory of cognitive dissonance. Stanford

University Press, Stanford, CA.

Fischhoff, B. (1975). Hindsight - foresight: The effect of outcome knowledge on judgement under uncertainty, Journal of experimental psychology: Human Perception and Performance, 1: 288-299.

Fischhoff, B. (1975a). Hindsight: Thinking backward, Psychology Today, 8: 71-76.

Fischhoff, B. (1977). Cognitive liabilities and product liability, Journal of Product Liability, 1: 207-220.

Fishbein, M. and I. Ajzen (1975). Belief, attitude, intention and behavior: An introduction to theory and research. Addison-Wesley, Reading, M.A.

Fisher, R., W. Ury and B. Patton (1991). Getting to Yes. Business Books, London.

Fiske, S.T. and S.E. Taylor (1984). Social Cognition. Addison-Wesley, Reading, MA.

Garfinkel, H. (1967). Studies in Ethnomethodology. Polity Press, New York.

Ginsberg, A. (1990). Connecting diversification to performance: A sociocognitive approach, Academy of Management Review, 15, pp. 514-535.

Grant, R.M. (1988). On dominant logic, relatedness and the link between diversity and performance, Strategic Management Journal, 9 (6) pp. 639-642.

Grzelak, J.L. (1982). Preferences and cognitive processes in interdependence situations: A theoretical analysis of cooperation. In, V.J. Derlega and J. Grzelak (eds.), Cooperation and helping behavior: Theories and research (95-122). Academic Press, New York.

Hastie, R. (1981). Schematic principles in human memory. In, E.T. Higgins, C.P. Heimen and M.P. Zanna (eds.). Social cognition: The Ontario Symposium. Erlbaum, Hallsdale, N.J.

Hatfield, E. and S. Sprecher (1986). The Importance of Looks in Everyday Life: Mirror, Mirror. State University of New York Press, New York

Hovland, C.I., I.L. Janis and H.H. Kelley (1953). Communication and persuation: Psychological studies of opinion change. Yale University Press, New Haver, C.T.

Kahneman, D.E. and A. Tversky (1972). Subjective probability: A judgment of representativeness, Cognitive Psychology, 3: 430-454.

Kahneman, D. and A. Tversky (1973). On the psychology of prediction, Psychological Review, 80: 237-251.

Kelley, H.H. (1950). The warm-cold variable in first impressions of persons, Journal of Personality, 18: 431-439.

Kenrick, D.T. and S.E. Guitierres (1980). Contrast effects in judgements of attractiveness: When beauty becomes a social problem, Journal of Personality and Social Psychology, 38: 131-140.

Kenrich, D.T., S.E. Gutierres and L.L. Goldberg (1989). Influence of popular erotica on judgements of strangers and mates, Journal of Experimental Social Psychology, 25: 159-167.

Kleinke, C.L. and R.A. Staneski (1980). First impressions of female bust size, Journal of Social Psychology, 110: 123-134.

Kunz, R.R. and M. Woolcott (1976). Season´s greetings: From my status to yours, Social Science Research, 5: 269-278.

Langer, E.J. (1989). Minding matters. In L. Berkowitz (Ed.). Advances in Experimental Social Psychology, Vol. 22. Academic Press, New York.

Langer, E.J., B. Blank and C. Chanowitz (1978). Rethinking the role of thought in social interaction. In J.H. Harvey, W.J. Ickes and R.F. Kidd (eds.). New Directions in Attribution Research, Vol. 2. Halstead Press, New York.

Lasswell, H.D. (1948). The Structure and Function of Communication in Society. In L.Bryson (Ed.). The Communication of Ideas: Religion and civilization series (37-51). Harper & Row, New York.

Latané, B. (1981). The Psychology of Social impact, American Psychologist, 36: 343-356.

Lax, D.A. and J.K. Sebenius (1986). The Manager as Negotiator. Free Press, London.

Luhmann, N. (1986). The autopoiesis of social systems. In F. Geyer and J. van der Zouwen (eds.). Sociocybernetic Paradoxes. Sage. Beverly Hills, CA. pp. 172-192.

Luhmann, N. (1992). Ecological Communication. Polity Press. Cambridge.

Lyles, M.A. and C.R. Schwenk. (1992). Top management, strategy and organizational knowledge structures, Journal of Management Studies, 29, pp. 155-174.

Lynn, M. (1989). Scarcity effect on value: Mediated by assumed expensiveness, Journal of Economic Psychology, 10: 257-274.

Markus, H. and S. Zajonic (1985). Cognitive Theories in Social psychology. In G. Lindzey and E. Aronseon (Eds.). Handbook of Social psychology. Vol. 1 : 137-230. Addison-Wesley, Reading, MA.

McGuire, W.J. (1972). Attitude change: The information-processing paradigm. In C.G. McClintock (Ed.). Experimental social psychology (108-141). Holt, Reinhort & Winston, New York.

McGuire, W.J. (1985). Attitudes and attitude change. In G. Lindzey & E. Aronson (eds.), Handbook of sosial psychology, Vol. 2 (233-346). Random House, New York.

Milgram, S. (1974). Obedience to Authority. Harper & Row, New York.

Miller, J.G. (1978). Living Systems. McGraw-Hill, New York.

Nisbett, R.E. and L. Ross (1980). Human inference: Strategies and shortcomings of social judgement. Prentice Hall, Englewood Cliffs, N.J.

Northcraft, G.B. and G. Wolfe (1984). Dollars, sense and sunk costs: A life cycle model of resource allocation decisions, Academy of management Review, 9: 225-234.

Peters, D.P. and S.J. Ceci (1982). Peer-review practices of the psychological journals: The fate of published chapters, submitted again, The Behavior and Brain Sciences, 5: 187-195.

Pitz, G.F. (1974). Subjective probability distributions for imperfectly known quantities. In L.W. Gregg (Ed.). Knowledge and cognition (29-41). John Wiley, New York.

Prahalad, C.K. and R.A. Bettis (1986). The dominant logig: A new linkage between diversity and performance, Strategic Management Journal, 7(6) pp. 485-501.

Pruitt, D.G. and P.J. Carnevale (1993). Negotiation in social conflict. Open University Press, Buckingham.

Raiffa, H. (1982). The Art and Science of Negotiation. Harvard University Press, Cambridge, Mass.

Ramanujam, V. and P. Varadarajan (1989). Research on corporate diversification: A synthesis, Strategic Management Journal, 10 (6) pp. 523-552.

Riley, D. and J. Eckenrode (1986). Social ties: Subgroup differences in cost and benefits, Journal of Personality and Social Psychology, 51: 770-778.

Rosenfeld, P., J.G. Kennedy and R.A. Giacalone (1986). Decisionmaking: A demonstration of the postdecision dissonance effect, Journal of Social Psychology, 126: 663-665.

Ross, A.S. (1971). Effects of increased responsibility on bystander intervention: The presence of children, Journal of Personality and Social Psychology, 19: 306-310.

Ross, J. and B.M. Staw (1986). Expo 86: An escalation prototype, Administrative science quarterly, 31: 274-297.

Ross, M.B. and J. Salvia (1975). Attractiveness as a biasing factor in teaching judgments, American Journal of Mental Deficiency, 80: 96-98.

Rucker, M., D. Taber and A. Harrison (1981). The effect of clothing variation and first impressions of female job applicants; what to wear when, Social Behavior and Personality, 9: 53-64.

Ruesch, J. and G. Bateson (1951). Communication: The Social Matrix of Psychiatry. W.W. Norton, New York.

Sheppard, B.H., J. Hartwick and P.R. Warshaw (1988). The Theory of Reasoned Action: A meta-Analysis of Past Research With Recommendations for Modifications and Future Research, Journal of Consumer Research, 15: 325-343.

Slovic, P. and S. Lichtenstein (1971). Comparison of Bayesian and regression approaches in the study of information processing in judgement, Organizational Behavior and Human Performance, 6: 649-744.

Smith, D.L., D.G. Pruitt and P.J. Carnevale (1982). Matching and Mismatching: The effect of own limit, others toughness and time pressure on concession rate in negotiation, Journal of Personality and Social Psychology, 42: 876-883.

Starbuch, W.H. (1983). Organizations as action generators, American Sociological Review, vol. 48: 91-102.

Stephan, W. (1984). Intergroup relations. In E.Aronson and G.Lindzey (Eds.). Handbook of Social Psychology, Vol. 2, pp. 599-658. Addison-Wesley, Reading, MA.

Staw, B.M. and J. Ross (1980). Commitment in an experimenting society: An experiment on the attribution of leadership from administrative scenarios, Journal of Applied Psychology, 65: 249-260.

Tanford, S. and S. Penrod (1983). Computer modeling of influence on the jury: The role of the consistent jurer, Social psychology Quarterly, 46: 200-212.

Tesser, A. (1978). Self-generated attitude change. In L. Berkowitz (Ed.). Advances in Experimental Social Psychology, Vol. 11. Academic Press, New York.

Thompson, L.L. (1991). Information exchange in negotiation, Journal of experimental Social Psychology, 27: 161-179.

Tversky, A. and D. Kahneman (1971). The belief in the law of numbers. Psychological Bulletin, 76: 105-110.

Tversky, A. & Kahneman, D. (1973). Availability: A heuristic for judging frequency and probability, Cognitive Psychology, 5: 207-232.

Tversky, A. and D. Kahneman (1974). Judgement under uncertainty: Heuristics and biases, Science, 185: 1124-1131.

Tversky, A. and D. Kahneman (1983). Extensional versus intuitive reasoning: The conjunction fallacy in probability judgment, Psychological Review, 90: 293-315.

Von Krogh, G., J. Roos and K. Slocum (1994). An Essay on Corporate Epistemology, Strategic Management Journal, Vol. 15: 53-71.

Warchel, S. (1992). Beyond a commodity theory analysis of censorship: When abundance and personalism enhance scarcity effects, Basic and Applied Social Psychology, 13: 79-93.

Wason, P.C. (1960). On the failure to eliminate hypotheses in a conceptual task, Quarterly Journal of Experimental Psychology, 12: 129-140.

Wason, P.C. (1968). Reason about a rule, Quarterly Journal of Experimental Psychology, 20: 273-283.

Wason, P.C. (1968a). On the failure to eliminate hypothesis: A second look. In P.C. Wason and P.N. Johnson Laird (eds.). Thinking and Reasoning. Penguin, Harmandsworth.

Wilson, P. (1983). Second-Hand Knowledge: An Inquiry into cognitive Authority. Greenwood Press, New York.

Yukl, G.A. (1974). The effects of situational variables and opponent concessions on bargainers perception, aspiration, and concessions, Journal of Personality and social Psychology, 29: 237-236.

Zubek, J.M., D.G. Pruitt, R.S. Peirce, N.B. McGillicaddy and H. Syna (1992). Short term success in mediation: Its relationship to disputant and mediator behaviors and prior conditions. Journal of Conflict Resolution, 36: 546-572.

Chapter 3 Prospect theory in negotiations: Influencing the Situation

Introduction

The problem under investigation is people's resistance to organizational change (Griffin & Moorhead, 2014; Harvey, 2010; Evans, 2001). This chapter investigates the following question: How can prospect theory be used to explain why people resist organizational change? The chapter aims to identify how managers can reduce resistance to change in i.e. negotiation processes. It also aims to identify explanations of why people resist organizational change. The key concept of this investigation is how people relate to particular risks that they are experiencing in negotiation situations.

Risk relates to our assumptions about potential outcomes and how these outcomes are evaluated by the decision-maker(s) in question (Pollatsek & Tversky, 1970, p. 541; Elster, 1986). Prospect theory was developed by Kahneman and Tversky in 1979 (Kahneman & Tversky, 1979). The theory holds that when people are faced with a risk about which they have limited information, and do not apply rigorous analytical processes, their choices will often be driven by how the information about the situation is framed either by themselves or others (Wolfe, 2008, p. 6).

The core idea of prospect theory is that people make assessments based on what they may gain or lose as the result of making a choice. One example of such a choice might be whether or not to engage actively in a change process within an organization. According to prospect theory, the possibility of losing an existing position will generate a level of resistance that will outweigh the energy and resources a person might expend in order to gain a new position (Kahneman, 2011, pp. 279-280). Most people are averse to losing something that they have already gained.

People's assessments are largely biased, distorted and not wholly reliable. Regardless of this fact, people make considerable use of these assessments in decision-making. Tversky and Kahneman found in the course of the research that led them to develop prospect theory that these assessments were heuristics or "rules of thumb" that people use in decision-making (Tversky & Kahneman, 1974, 1983). A basic assumption in prospect theory is that people use these rules of thumb without even realizing that they are doing so.

The content of this chapter is summarized in Fig. 1, which also shows how the chapter is structured. This chapter also includes a separate section that explains concrete measures that may be taken by management. These measures are based on the seven propositions developed during the course of this chapter.

Fig. 1: Prospect theory as an explanation of why people resist organizational change in negotiation.

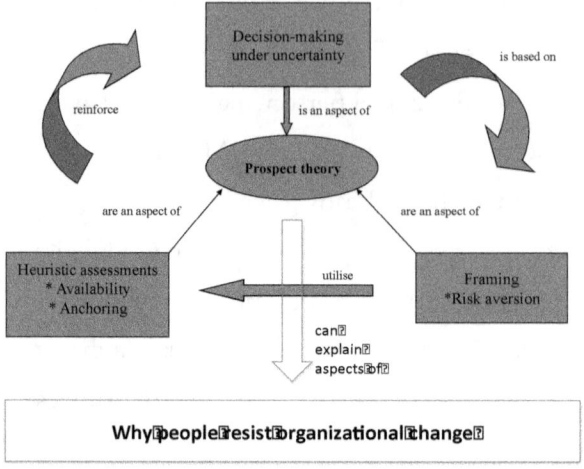

Literature review: Decision-making under uncertainty

At first, it may seem reasonable to assume that people will seek out risk if they are living under poor conditions. This assumption concludes that the situation can't get worse, so people will take risks in order to improve their life situation. According to prospect theory, however, this intuitive assumption is incorrect. In fact, when a person faces the possibility of losing the rights, power, positions, income, etc., that he or she has already achieved, they will seek to retain what they have achieved and are reluctant to change (Kahneman & Tversky, 2000, p. 22). People avoid participating in change processes for as long as possible because they risk losing what they have achieved.

The explanation of why people are risk-averse is linked to what is known in prospect theory as the "certainty effect" (Kahneman & Tversky,

2000, p. 17). Very broadly, this effect can be described as a preference for the certain over the possible.

What is different about prospect theory, in contrast to, for example, rational choice theory (Kahneman, 2011), is that prospect theory takes account of how we will act both when we face the loss of rights, positions, etc., and when we face the possibility of gaining the same kinds of rights, positions, etc.

If one is in a situation where one risks losing positions one has gained, one will be willing to take a risk in order to retain one's current position. If one faces a situation where one has an expectation of gain, then the probability is great (paradoxically) that one will prefer to secure what one has already achieved.

Prospect theory uses the phrase "reference point" to denote the point at which we take action in the various situations described above. Our assessment of a situation is determined by the position we are in when we undertake the process of assessing the situation. The key psychological concept of prospect theory is that people dislike the idea of losing a position but like the idea of winning one (Kahneman, 2011, p. 281). The important point here, however, is that people will commit more effort to preventing a loss than achieving a potential gain (Kahneman & Tversky, 2000, p. 22). In addition, Kahneman and Tversky state that people's commitment increases when they are trying to prevent a loss but decreases when they are trying to gain something (Kahneman & Tversky, 2000, p. 17). For all practical purposes, this means that the energy and resources a person will use to prevent a loss will increase in proportion to the likely size of the loss. The converse is not true in respect of a gain.

Proposition 1. If management structures their change project to take account of the fact that people will resist change because they risk losing what they have already achieved, then the change project will have a greater chance of success.

Practical implications. People will expend more energy and resources on preventing losses than on gaining new positions.

Negotiation implications. Management should be aware that if employees face a situation that offers a potential benefit then the likelihood is great that they will prefer instead to secure their existing positions.

The "reflection effect" reverses the "certainty effect". As a rule of thumb, resistance to change is reversed when the possible gains are between 1.5 and 2.5 times greater than the status quo (Kahneman, 2011, p. 284). It is when gains reach this point that participation in organizational changes comes into consideration. This concerns when one can choose between retaining that which is established and secure on the one hand, and investing resources in a process of change on the other. The choice will, in the context of the "reflection effect", be related to the expectation of future opportunities to choose to participate in change, rather than to retaining a reliable and proven solution.

A third psychological effect that prospect theory refers to is the "isolation effect" (Kahneman & Tversky, 2000, p. 17). This refers to people's tendency to discard elements that all choice situations have in common, leading to inconsistent preferences. The focus in this context is on what separates the choice options, i.e. that which creates a distinction (Tversky, 1972). Among other things, this effect means that choice options are broken down and framed in terms of a probability of loss or possibility of gain. If a change situation is presented as involving a probable loss, then one will maintain the status quo. However, if the change is presented as an opportunity to make very large gains, say more than 100 per cent of what one already has, then it will be possible to apply the certainty effect and the reflection effect to move someone from a status quo situation to a situation involving investment and commitment to a change project. Presenting information in this way means that people are willing to change, even if they do not have complete information about the outcome.

Fig. 2 shows a model of how the three effects (certainty effect, reflection effect and isolation effect) can vary in relation to each other, explaining resistance to change during organizational changes.

Fig. 2: Resistance to change in organizations.

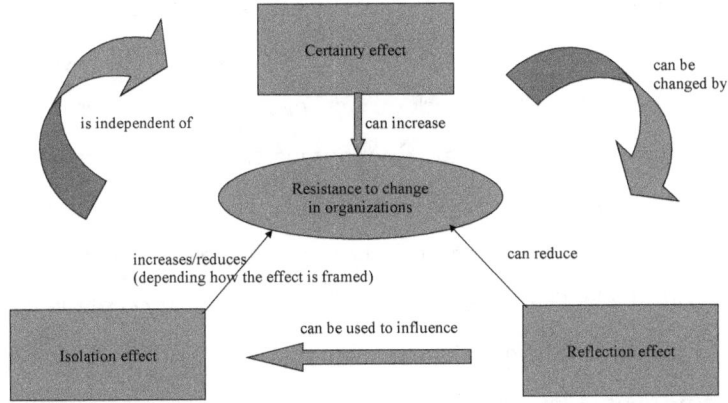

In prospect theory, psychological assessments are related to three elements: losing, winning and the reference point (McDermott, 2001). The reference point is, as a rule, related to expectations or the status quo (Kahneman, 2011, p. 282). What is perceived by some as a large gain may be perceived by others as insignificant (Vis, 2010).

In prospect theory, there is always a reference point related to expectations about a possible gain. This is the basis for assessing whether to seek to secure what you already have or to seek any changes that present themselves.

The practical choices are often complex and involve a risk of loss and a possibility of gain. Consequently, we operate, in effect, with a subjective assessment of expected usefulness in relation to our choices. There are risks and uncertainties associated with choices: the choices are often not that clear-cut and frequently include mixed assessments.

A useful rule of thumb for managers that can encourage people to engage in an organizational change project is to be aware that the expected gains must be about 100 per cent or more in relation to the status quo. The tendency will then be to choose the option for potential gains in spite of the fact that there is still the possibility of loss (Vis, 2010). Experiments have shown that the rate of loss aversion increases with increasing investment, so the more that is at stake, the greater the possibility of gain must also be if one is to choose to fully embark on a change project (McDermott, 2001). However, the loss aversion rate does not increase proportionally with the possibility of loss. For instance, in situations where life is threatened or people are exposed to bankruptcy, the degree of loss aversion is dramatically high. There are certain actions that are unacceptable no matter what the possible final gain (Kahneman, 2011, p. 284). This may explain why some people enter into organizational change processes while others don't. In practice, the degree of loss aversion can be much greater for some people depending on their life experiences (Vis, 2010). For instance, individuals and groups accustomed to experiencing losses, such as professional gamblers, military officers, financial brokers, vulnerable and marginalized groups, etc., may have a greater tolerance of losses.

Proposition 2. If management presents the changes as an opportunity to achieve a gain of more than 100 per cent of what employees already have (the status quo), then it is highly probable that employees will consider the change project as positive.

Practical implications. If management wants to reduce resistance to change, then they should present the possible gain as being more than 100 per cent.

Negotiation implications. Management can reduce resistance to change in organizations by taking advantage of the interaction between the certainty effect, the reflection effect, and the isolation effect.

Literature review: Framing

Prospect theory assumes that people do not act on the basis of full information when making decisions. They instead usually act on the basis of available information. Following from this, the theory does *not* assume that people are fully rational when making choices. The theory investigates how people act in practice when making choices, asking, for example, how they use intuition when making choices in uncertain situations. When faced with a choice between an uncertain change that may offer future opportunities and a current status quo situation, people often act on the basis of the proverb "A bird in the hand is worth two in the bush". In other words, we tend to choose the safe option over the one which is uncertain but which offers opportunities.

Some people also tend to be optimistic about any given situation they find themselves in. Such a bias is both a blessing and a risk, says Kahneman (Kahneman, 2011, p. 255). The so-called "pessimists" and "optimists" have been examined and discussed in several empirical studies (Seligman, 2006; Snowdon, 2001; Fox, Ridgewell, & Ashwin, 2009). The optimists, Kahneman writes, are "…the inventors, the entrepreneurs. …They got to where they are by seeking challenges and taking risks" (Kahneman, 2011, p. 256). Although most of us are risk-averse, some of us are optimists and willing to participate in change processes even though expectations do not offer 100 per cent or greater gains regarding the possible outcome.

Proposition 3. If management discovers who the optimists are and assigns them to the change project, then the probability is great that the change project will succeed.

Practical implications. We tend to opt for that which is established and safe and discard the opportunity for potential gains. This conservative element in human decision-making may also partly explain why there is a time lag between an assumed necessary change and the impact of change in the organization.

Negotiation implications. It is easier to involve the optimists in a change project than the pessimists. Management should therefore search for optimists and let them be the agents of change for the project.

It is the framing aspect of prospect theory that has received most attention (Wolfe, 2008, p. 9). Framing can be understood as the way in which "individuals and groups make sense of their external environment" (Boettcher, 2004, p. 331). We use framing to organize and understand the world around us. Using information frames, we are able to perceive a phenomenon, issue, event, etc., in a new way. Prospect theory argues that framing is used to make choices and assumptions in relation to future outcomes (Tversky & Kahneman, 1981). How information concerning our choices is presented is an important consideration in the framing phase of prospect theory (McDermott, 2001, p. 21). We can also frame that which is rational so that it appears reasonable, even though something that is rationally justified might not necessarily have a reasonable justification.

Sense and rationality can be contradictory terms, although they may also be congruent.

The most general part of framing in prospect theory concerns how a loss is framed in relation to a gain. This may be achieved by selecting information frames that result in the loss or gain appearing in a different light to an individual.

Losses and gains are considered in relation to the status quo and what will serve one's own interests or those of the system (Mandel, 2001). The framing or editing of a given situation may be termed prospect theory's initial phase (McDermott, 2001, p. 20). In many situations we are not aware of what opportunities exist or the possible outcomes of our choices. Consequently, we often construct possible alternatives and the results of pursuing them before making a decision; this is the creative aspect in any decision-making process. It is during this stage that management should think through the importance of which information frames they will use. In other words, according to prospect theory we adopt a kind of bias. We have an aversion to losing what we have already gained; therefore, our choices will be influenced by how the choices and the prospective results of these choices are framed. How the information framework is used is consequently not an insignificant part of the outcome of how people react to change projects in organizations.

Tversky and Kahneman express this clearly by saying that "…choice depends on the status quo, or reference level: changes of reference point lead to reversals of preference" (Tversky & Kahneman, 2000, p. 143). In our context, this can explain the importance of how information frameworks are presented in relation to the extent of resistance to change in organizations.

One of the principal assumptions of prospect theory that emphasizes the importance of information frames is that "losses and disadvantages have greater impact on preferences than gains and advantages" (Tversky & Kahneman, 2000, p. 143). Loss aversion in prospect theory has major implications for how people in organizations relate to change and how their preferences change when reference points shift over time. Information frames are concerned with moving the reference point, not providing valid information that is completely reliable.

Proposition 4. If management frames information concerning the change project as representing a large gain for everyone, then the probability is great that employees will consider the change project in a positive light.

Practical implications. The assumption here is that it is people's perception of the reference point that will move them in one direction or the other.

Negotiation implications. Management should be cautious about introducing too many changes simultaneously and carrying out rapid changes in succession because this may easily lead to erratic behavior in organizations. This can lead to a loss of efficiency and increased resistance to change projects in the organization.

Literature review: Heuristic assessments

There are four basic heuristic assessments that Tversky and Kahneman have described (Beach & Connolly, 2005, pp. 81-83; Kahneman, 2011; Tversky & Kahneman, 1974, 1983). These are:

1. Representativeness and randomness,
2. Anchoring
3. Availability
4. Validity.

In this chapter, only anchoring and availability will be discussed because these are the most relevant in explaining why people oppose change in organizations.

Anchoring. A boat at anchor can move around, but the anchorage will always be its pivot point. To move the anchor point, you have to take up the anchor and physically move it to another place. If you have first dropped anchor, then you have also chosen the pivot point or the point around which negotiations will revolve. The anchor effect does not concern a lack of or incorrect information; it is an effect that seems to apply even if we have sufficient information (Chapman & Johnson, 2002). When we are trying to estimate something, such as the probable success of a change project, the development of property prices (Northcraft & Neale, 1987), the benefits of adopting a new idea in an organizational change project, etc., we will often begin by making an initial estimate. This is our so-called "anchor". We will then make adjustments in relation to the anchor (Beach & Connolly, 2005, pp. 82-83). However, if the anchor is not placed correctly, then the probability is great that the final results will also differ from what was originally planned. This calls to mind a popular quotation from Ibsen's *Peer Gynt*: "But when the starting point is weakest the result is often the most original".

Thus, according to prospect theory, where you set the anchor in relation to a prospect will affect subsequent behavior (Kahneman, 2011, p. 119). Whether one chooses to invest in a change project is also related to the anchor of how project information is framed, i.e. the risk in relation to winning or losing what has already been gained. If you take the risk of investing in a change project, how much is the potential upside? We have seen above that the potential upside should be more than 100 per cent. However, experiments have also shown that the gain should range between as much as 150 and 250 per cent if one is to take the risk of investing in something new. It is the anchor related to risk aversion that is interesting from a change perspective, because it says something about how willing the individual is to engage in a change project.

An interesting aspect from an information perspective is that people consider their potential gains and losses from the anchor that has been set even when it has been set randomly (Chapman & Johnson, 2002:120-138). It appears that the anchor effect operates in such a way that the end result on average does not vary by more than 55 per cent from the anchor that was originally set. In experiments, this seems to apply even if the anchor is not taken into account (Kahneman, 2011:124). From an information perspective, this is important knowledge for management or those who are selling a change project.

An interesting point related to anchors is that they affect us, although we are aware of this (Wilson & Brekke, 1994:117-142). Anchors are used to extract and select information, integrate this information and then formulate a response to another party (Chapman & Johnson, 2002, p. 126). This says something about the strength of the anchor effect.

Proposition 5. If management uses the anchor effect to control people's resistance to change, then the probability is great that employees will engage positively in the change project.

Practical implications. The anchor effect explains aspects of why people oppose changes in organizations and may be used to reduce people's resistance to change.

Negotiation implications. Management should be aware of the fact that the anchor effect may differ by 55 per cent from a set anchor.

Availability. If information is available at regular intervals, then it is easy to refer to such information (Beach & Connolly, 2005, p. 82). We say in such situations that the information is available in one's memory. However, it is not only information that is often repeated that is available for retrieval in one's memory; events that have left a deep impression also have the same availability effect. For instance, emotional childhood experiences, air disasters, genocide, pestilence, economic crises, change projects that went wrong resulting in mass dismissals, etc., are easier to recall from memory than, for example, the fact that thousands of people are killed every year in traffic accidents.

It is therefore understandable that journalists, historians, and others compare the 2008 economic crisis with the 1930s depression because examples from the 1930s depression can easily be retrieved from memory. However, it is dangerous to make such a comparison if the 1930s depression can only to a small extent be relevantly compared to the 2008 economic crisis. If politicians initiate measures for the recent economic crisis on the basis of knowledge of initiatives that should have been adopted in the 1930s, this may create more problems than it solves. This example says something about the importance of information availability.

The question "Why do we believe more in one type of information than in another type?" may, among other things, be answered by the fact that some types of information are easier to retrieve from memory than others. In other words, the information we believe in is more "true" than other types of information. In this context, the expression "availability cascades" used by Kuran and Sunstein (Kuran & Sunstein, 1999) is of interest. By this they mean that we are to a certain extent controlled by the image of reality that is constructed by the media because it is easier to retrieve from memory. How easily information may be retrieved from memory when faced with a situation demonstrates the availability proposition's relevance. The availability proposition can be expressed in the following way: the more easily information enters into our consciousness, the greater the likelihood that we will have confidence in that information. In other words, we believe more in the type of information that is available in the memory than information that is not so readily available.

What is important to note concerning the availability proposition is that information does not necessarily need to be credible as long as it is available. It is, inter alia, in such contexts that Kahneman asks us to use System 2 (Kahneman, 2011), which he uses to refer to analytical thinking to check the validity of information. However, it is the availability proposition that prevails, because most people are not trained in statistics and analysis of information.

Proposition 6. If management uses the information available in the memory of employees and develops an anchor in relation to this information, then the probability is great that employees will consider the change project in a positive light.

Practical implications. We have a tendency to distort information and believe that the information that is easier to retrieve from memory is more credible than information that emerges after thorough analysis.

Negotiation implications. Management should use information about change projects that can easily be compared with historical or contemporary events that employees can easily identify with.

A variation of the availability proposition is the affect proposition, which concerns how emotionally affected you are by the situation that is being assessed. In other words, the perceived risk of a project may be reduced if you are more emotionally affected by the project. In the real world, "we often face painful trade-offs between benefits and costs" (Kahneman, 2011, p. 140). Whether you choose to engage in a change project or prefer the status quo may depend on how emotionally affected you are by the project.

Proposition 7. If management succeeds in getting employees emotionally involved in the change process, then the probability is great that they will consider the perceived risk associated with such changes as small.

Practical implications. Whether people are willing to engage in a change project or try to preserve the status quo may depend on the extent to which they experience changes as emotionally attractive.

Negotiation implications. To increase the emotional reward of a change, it seems reasonable to assume that management should use the anchor effect and framing.

Specific measures that management can implement

On the basis of the seven propositions described above, the following measures may be considered to reduce resistance to change in organizations.

Decision-making under uncertainty

Risk aversion. As a general rule, people seek to retain what they have already gained and are reluctant to change. We often operate on the basis of intuitive rules and psychological principles that govern the framing of information about our choices. However, these rules and principles are not necessarily rational or logical.

Management can apply this knowledge in order to reduce resistance to change by:

1. Crisis understanding: point out the necessity of the changes.

2. Psychological safety: point out that the proposed changes do not carry any risk of loss for employees.
3. Expectation management: point out the benefits of the changes.

The potential must be more than 100 per cent. There are three effects that may be employed in efforts to reduce resistance to change in organizations. The first is called the "certainty effect". This implies that one chooses what is certain, i.e. what you already have, rather than that which is probable and offers opportunities, such as engaging in an organizational change project where the outcome is uncertain. The second effect is called the "reflection effect", which reverses the "certainty effect" if there are expectations of future gains of more than 100 per cent stemming from the change. The third effect is called the "isolation effect", which refers to a tendency to discard elements that all choices have in common and to focus on what separates the choices (Kahneman & Tversky, 2000, p. 17).

Management may increase the likelihood that employees will engage with and dedicate themselves to a change project by presenting the changes in such a way that they will lead to improvements in the proposition to employees that accrue to gains of more than 100 per cent across a number of change proposal elements.

Framing

We seek safety. We have a tendency to be conservative in our thinking: we wish to retain that which we have and are reluctant to adopt that which is new. One way for management to engage with this conservative aspect of our thinking may be to engage those who have little risk aversion in relation to the change project as project managers at various levels. The rationale for this strategy is provided by Kahneman. The people who are responsible for the implementation of a change project are often more optimistic than those who are not in this position, and optimists are more positive about change than pessimists. Kahneman underlines this supposition with the following statement: "…the people who have the greatest influence on the lives of others are likely to be optimistic and overconfident, and to take more risks than they realize" (Kahneman, 2011, p. 256).

Management should identify the optimists in the organization because they will most likely participate in the change project even though the possible future gain is not more than 100 per cent. They should also identify the sceptics to the change project and give them responsibility for some of the changes.

Erratic behavior. If management introduces too many consecutive changes this can easily result in the organization becoming unsettled. Consequently, employees may become reluctant to accept more changes. This may result in alienating those who initially supported the need for change and give more weight to those who are opposed to change.

Management may prevent such erratic behavior by involving employees at an early stage in the planning of changes. In the planning phase they should frame information so that the change project is presented as a win-win solution, where employees make large gains and risk losing little. In this way everyone is informed about what must be done, why it should be done, how it should be done, and the desired effects of the changes.

Heuristic assessments

Anchoring. Use of the anchor effect for strategic purposes can result in us making choices we would not normally make. Countless experiments have shown that people's choices correspond to the anchor they use, even though the anchor may be irrelevant, random and evidently incorrectly set (Epley & Gilovich, 2002, p. 139). If you have a strong expectation of future success, then this expectation, this anchor, influences your behavior in the present (Switzer & Sniezek, 1991). Taking into account the anchor effect can help reduce resistance to change in organizations (Tversky & Kahneman, 1974). Moreover, it is advantageous to frame your project with a possible future gain of 150–250 per cent in relation to the status quo. An important point concerning the anchor effect is that it controls our behavior, even though we have sufficient information about the situation.Management can use this insight by setting the anchor in such a way that expectations are motivating for the individual.

Availability. The availability proposition developed by Tversky and Kahneman in 1972–1973 (Kahneman, 2011, p. 129) can be expressed in the following simplified form: the easier information is to retrieve from memory, the greater the cognitive authority that information has. If you want to sell a change project, then it can be advantageous to link it to a media event that has a positive connotation.

Management can reduce resistance to change by linking the change project to a media event that has a strong positive connotation (cascade effect).

Emotional strength. One relies more on information that reinforces our perception of the object, event or action if we are emotionally attracted to the object. When this happens we will take greater risks, and we will have a tendency to assign less importance to information that is critical and rely more on information that is positively charged in relation to the change project.

Management should encourage employees to become emotionally connected to the change project because this will trigger individual commitment and dedication to change.

Conclusion

In this chapter we have attempted to answer the following question: how can we use prospect theory to explain why people resist organizational change? To answer this question seven propositions have been developed.

There are three magnitudes around which the propositions are organized. These are: decision-making under uncertainty, framing, and heuristic assessments (anchoring and availability).

In Decision-making under uncertainty there are two propositions. Proposition one is related to the knowledge that if people risk losing what they have already achieved, they will resist change. Proposition two says that the probability is high that employees will consider the change project as positive, if they think they achieve a gain of more than 100 per cent of what one already has (the status quo).

In Framing there are also two propositions. The first proposition in framing tells management to discovers who the optimists are, and assigns them to the change project. If they do so, then the probability is great that the change project will succeed. The second proposition in framing says that management ought to frame information concerning the change project as representing a large gain for everyone. If they do so, then the probability is great that employees will consider the change project in a positive light.

In Heuristic assessments there are three propositions in two categories: anchoring and availability. We have one proposition in Anchoring. This propositions states that if management uses the anchor effect to control people's resistance to change, then the probability is great that employees will engage positively with the change project.

We have two propositions in availability. The first proposition states that if management uses the information available in the memory of employees, and develops an anchor in relation to this information, then the probability is great that employees will consider the change project in a positive light. The second proposition in availability tells that if management succeeds in getting employees emotionally involved in the change process, then the probability is great that they will consider the perceived risk associated with such changes as small.

Taken together the seven proposition have been compiled into a system, defined here as a "mini-theory", about how resistance to organizational change can be reduced. For each of the seven propositions we have discussed practical and Negotiation implications.

References

Adriaenssen, D.J., & Johannessen, J.-A. (2015). Conceptual generalisation: Methodological reflections in social science, a systemic viewpoint. *Kybernetes*: *The International Journal of Cybernetics, Systems and Management Sciences*,44,4:588

605.

Beach, L.R., & Connolly, T. (2005). *The psychology of decision making: People in organizations.* London: Sage.

Boettcher, W.A. (2004). The prospects for prospect theory: An empirical evaluation of international relations applications of framing and loss aversion. *Political Psychology, 25 (3),* 331-362.

Bunge, M. (1974). *Sense and reference.* Dordrecht: Reidel.

Bunge, M. (1998). *Philosophy of science: From problem to theory: Vol. 1.* New Brunswick, NJ: Transaction.

Bunge, M. (1999). *The sociology-philosophy connection.* New Brunswick, NJ: Transaction.

Bunge, M. (2001). *Philosophy in crisis: The need for reconstruction.* Amherst, NY: Prometheus Books.

Chapman, G.B., & Johnson, E.J. (2002). Incorporating the irrelevant: Anchors in judgments of belief and value. In T. Gilovich, D. Griffin & D. Kahneman (Eds.), *Heuristics and biases: The psychology of intuitive judgment* (pp. 120-138). Cambridge: Cambridge University Press.

Elster, J. (1986). *Rational choice.* New York: New York University Press.

Epley, N., & Gilovich, T. (2002). Putting adjustment back in the anchoring and adjustment heuristic. In T. Gilovich, D. Griffin & D. Kahneman (Eds.), *Heuristics and biases: The psychology of intuitive judgment* (pp. 139-149). Cambridge: Cambridge University Press.

Evans, R. (2001). *The human side of school change*. London: Jossey-Bass.

Fox, E., Ridgewell, A., & Ashwin, C. (2009). Looking on the bright side: Biased attention and the human serotonin transporter gene. *Proceedings of the Royal Society B, 276*, 1747-1751..

Griffin, R., & Moorhead, G. (2014). *Organizational behavior: Managing people and organizations* (pp. 543-546). Mason, OH: South Western Cengage Learning.

Harvey, T.R. (2010). *Resistance to change*. London: R & L Education.

Kahneman, D. (2011). *Thinking fast and slow*. New York: Allen Lane.

Kahneman, D., & Tversky, A. (1979). An analysis of decision under risk. *Econometrica, Journal of the Econometric Society, 47*(2), 263-292.

Kahneman, D., & Tversky, A. (2000). Prospect theory: An analysis of decision under risk. In D. Kahneman, & A. Tversky (Eds.), *Choices, values and frames* (pp. 17-43) Cambridge: Cambridge

University Press.

Kuran, T., & Sunstein, C.R. (1999). Availabilities cascades and risk regulation. *Stanford Law Review, 51*, 683-768.

Mandel, D.R. (2001). Gain-loss framing and choice: Separating outcome formulations from descriptor formulations. *Organizational Behavior and Human Decision Processes, 85 (1)*, 56-76.

Northcraft, G.B., & Neale, M.A. (1987). Experts, amateurs, and real estate: An anchoring-and-adjustment perspective on property pricing decisions. *Organizational Behavior and Human Decision Processes, 39*, 84-97.

Pollatsek, A., & Tversky, A. (1970). A theory of risk. *Journal of Mathematical Psychology, 7*, 540-553.

Seligman, M.E.P. (2006). *Learned optimism.* New York: Vintage Books.

Snowdon, D. (2001). *Aging with grace: What the nun study teaches us about leading longer, healthier, and more meaningful lives.* New York: Bantam Books.

Switzer, F., & Sniezek, J.A. (1991). Judgment processes in motivation: Anchoring and adjustment effects on judgment and behavior. *Organizational Behavior and Human Decision Processes, 49*, 208-229.

Tversky, A. (1972). Elimination by aspects: A theory of choice. *Psychological Review, 79*, 281-299.

Tversky, A., & Kahneman, D. (1974). Judgment under uncertainty: Heuristics and biases. *Science, 185*, 1124-1131.

Tversky, A., & Kahneman, D. (1981). The framing of decisions and the psychology of choice. *Science, 211*, 453-458.

Tversky, A., & Kahneman, D. (1983). Extensional versus intuitive reasoning. The conjunction fallacy in probability judgment. *Psychological Review, 90*, 293-315.

Tversky, A., & Kahneman, D. (2000). Loss aversion in riskless choice. In D. Kahneman, & A. Tversky (Eds.), *Choices, values and frames* (pp.143-158). Cambridge: Cambridge University Press.

Vis, B. (2010). *Politics of risk-taking* (pp. 109-133). Amsterdam: Amsterdam University Press.

Wilson, T.D. & Brekke, N. (1994). Mental contamination and mental correction: Unwanted influences on judgment and evaluations. *Psychological Bulletin, 116*, 117-142.

Wolfe, W.M. (2008). *Winning the war of words*. London: Praeger.

Chapter 4 Mastering influence and negotiation

Introduction

According to Greene (2012:1), we all contribute to creating the conditions that are determinative of our own and others' ability to feel a sense of mastery. In this chapter, we use the following terms to describe input factors for the process of promoting a sense of mastery: self-image, personal strengths, and powers of endurance. This insight is drawn from the works of authors including Dweck, (2012), Fredrickson (2014), Petterson (2012), Dutton, et al. (2009; 2010; 2011), Hefferon (2015) and Seligman (2006; 2011;2013).

In this chapter we describe, analyse and discuss how one may alter one's own ability to feel a sense of mastery. The purpose of the chapter is to explain how one may cultivate factors that contribute to one's ability to feel a sense of mastery, so that managers may gain a practical tool to help employees to improve their ability to feel a sense of mastery.

From an evolutionary point of view, we have mastered our environment by changing and adapting ourselves. This is the view of authors including Bandura (1977; 2001; 2006). This is only half the truth, however. To a greater and greater extent, we have been compelled to master the environment that we ourselves have created (Bednar, et al., 1989).

The issue that we explore below is as follows: How can managers establish workplace conditions conducive to facilitating a sense of mastery for employees?

The research questions that we investigate in order to answer this issue are the following:

1. How can managers make use of employees' *self-image* in order to promote a sense of mastery among employees in the workplace?
2. How can managers apply employee's *personal strengths* and *powers of endurance* in order to promote a sense of mastery among employees in the workplace?

Fig. 1 shows how rhe chapter is organized.

Fig. 1 Mastery

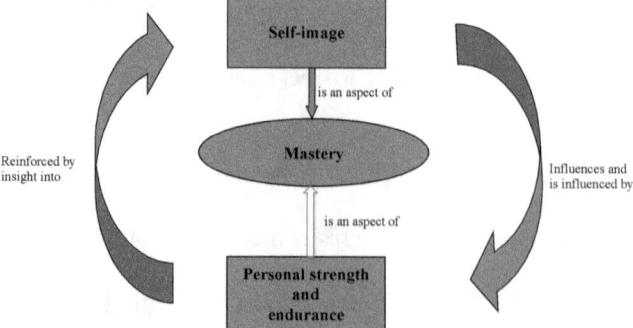

Self-image

According to Maddux (2009) and Mruk, (1999:1), self-image is significant to employees' general well-being and mental health. The status of a person's self-image will affect their behaviour. People with a positive self-image have been shown to be more adaptable (Bednar, et al., 1989). On the other hand, a poor self-image will contribute to feelings of inadequacy, issues with anxiety, increased sickness absence and other complex negative issues (Skager & Kerst, 1989). These will in turn negatively affect both levels of sickness absence (Robins, et al., 2008) and employees' performance. Both these issues will rapidly become of concern to managers.

The literature on psychology often considers the self to consist of two aspects: self-as-object and self-as-subject, or active agent (Robins et al., 2008). Our exposition and discussion will focus on the self as an active agent. A positive self-image corresponds with personal strength and resilience, says Maddux (2009).

Self-esteem may be defined as *the personal experience of how one copes in various areas and in various contexts, in relation to the expectations one has regarding how one should have coped* (Carr, 2011: 239). Mruk's model of self-esteem is constructed along two axes (Mruk, 1999: 164-165): one axis relates to the extent the individual feels he/she has the competence to tackle the tasks at hand; the other axis relates to the feeling the individual has regarding whether the contribution they are making is of any importance.

Some research shows that the self is formed in childhood, and changes very little after reaching the age of 30 (Robins, et al., 2008). In a management context, this means that a manager should deal with the self-esteem that employees already have, rather than trying to improve it. However, self-esteem may be improved in relation to the nature of the tasks at work, the organization of work and various feedback systems. In this context, it is important that managers design tasks for employees that they feel they master in order to get them to believe in themselves.

The self-image is maintained and enhanced through how the individual processes and uses information about themselves (Robins, et al., 2008). Although new information may emerge that could lead to the improvement of a poor self-image, then this information is distorted so that the individual maintains the self-image he/she has. The same applies to those who have a positive self-image and who receive information that really should have modified their perception of self in a negative direction (Carr, 2011).

A positive self-image is good for several reasons. People with a good self-image have better knowledge about themselves, set more appropriate goals, are more adaptable, implement the objectives they have set themselves, are more committed to completing a task, and they can cope better with criticism and negative feedback (Swam, et al., 2007).

A negative self-image is not good for several reasons. People with a negative self-image often have: poor adaptability; difficulty in maintaining stable relationships; a lower ability to cope with stress; a poorer immune system, a higher prevalence of depression, and a higher frequency of eating disorders and alcohol and drug abuse problems. These individuals also have higher absenteeism (Robins, et al., 2008).

No consistent view can be found in the research regarding the advantages and disadvantages of high versus low self-esteem (Baumeister, et al., 2003). However, most people agree that high self-esteem may be related to wellness and well-being, and that people with high self-esteem are more likely to take the initiative than those with low self-esteem (Baumeister, et al., 2003).

To improve the self-esteem of employees, it may be of advantage to consider the definitions of self-esteem as given above [Carr (2011:239) and Mruk (1999:164-165)]. On the basis of these two definitions, employees and managers may improve self-esteem in two ways. Firstly, this concerns what may be done regarding expectations; and, secondly, competence.

Competence may be improved by increasing knowledge related to the tasks that have to be carried out, skills training, as well as working with attitude changes where it seems appropriate. Research gives clear indications that employees' confidence is improved through a structured program (Haney & Durlak, 1998; Durlak, et al., 2010).

This chapter considers two aspects of self-esteem. The first is the strength of believing you can do a task, which, inter alia, Buckingham & Clifton (2005); Catman, et al., (2007: 464-467); Davidson, et al., (2000: 890-909) and Kempermann, et al., (1997: 493-495) have indicated is important for self-esteem. The second aspect we call self-regulation and adaptability, something, inter alia, Bandura (1977; 2001; 2006) has investigated in relation to self-efficacy. Each of these aspects will be explained, analysed and discussed in this section.

The above discussion is represented by Fig. 2.

Fig. 2 also shows how we have organized the description, analysis and discussion of self-esteem.

Fig. 2. Self-esteem: a cybernetic model

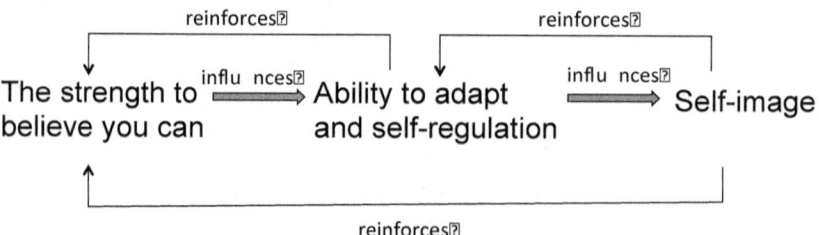

The strength of self-belief

The belief that one can do something, being positive and being active all add up to more than simply a good feeling. According to Cotman, et al. (2007: 464-472) and Davidson, et al., (2000:890-909), thinking in this way even impacts an individual's cells and neurons. It has been scientifically proven that being positive, active and believing that one can make something of one's future literally creates new resources right down to cellular level, while also boosting one's ability to resist external pressures. This has been shown by authors such as Kempermann, et al., (1997:493-495) and Maddux & Winstead (2015). The latest neuroscientific research shows active and positive behaviour promotes cellular renewal in both the body and the brain (Fredrickson, 2014:75;227). As pointed out by Seligman (2006; 2011;2013), the good news is that each and every one of us can boost our levels of positive thinking and behaviour (2006; 2011; 2013).

Bandura developed the "self-efficacy theory"; self-efficacy is concerned with the effect of believing in one's own ability to complete a task (Bandura, 1997: vii). In other words, the premise of the theory is that when you believe you have the necessary expertise to complete a task, then you will master the task better. The belief that you master a task also leads to you being able to adapt to changing circumstances, and being able to change behavioral strategies, which is also described by Asplund & Blacksmith (2013).

If you have faith in yourself, then the probability is high that you will have a high degree of mastery, and vice versa (Maddux, 2009:335). Challenges and opposition are also tackled better by people who believe they have the necessary expertise to manage a task (Bandura, 1977: vii). It is when the challenges change that belief in your own abilities come to expression. It is the belief that you have the necessary competence, and that you believe it means something that you contribute with your competence that is important in constituting self-esteem (Maddux, 2009:335).

Bandura's theory is not related to the intentions, motives, drive, need for control or expectations concerning results. The theory says only that if you think you have the necessary skills to perform a specific task, and you think you can make a difference, then it is highly probable you will be able to cope with the task (Bandura, 2001; 2006).

It is possible to develop the strength of believing you can. This concerns both children and adults. You can use the tools encompassed in the acronym GRIT (growth, resilience, integrity, tenacity) and "growth mindset" (Dweck, 2012). Psychologist Carol Dweck distinguishes between two ways of thinking. She designates the first a fixed mindset; the second a growth mindset (Dweck, 2012). We choose to consider mindfulness

(Langer, 2011: 279-293) as a sub-group of a growth mindset. Dweck's studies show that those with a growth mindset cope better than those with a fixed mindset.

People with a fixed mindset tend to believe that an individual's character traits, positive and negative, are innate and cannot be changed. Those who have a growth mindset believe change is possible, and therefore continuously try to learn from their own and others' mistakes. Therefore, those with a growth mindset are often those who work hard, persevere and achieve success. Managers can apply this knowledge about the differences between a fixed mindset and a growth mindset to promote employees sense of mastery.

Seligman (2011:102-125) discusses the research of Angela Lee Duckworth, a psychologist from Princeton. She has carried out studies over several years in various contexts using the question: *Who is successful here, and why?*[1] The answer she gives is that those people who are successful have so-called GRIT characteristics. What we can conclude from the research of Lee Duckworth and Dweck is that having belief in oneself is essential if one is

---

[1] Angela asks this question in a talk she gave about the key to success, where she explains the importance of GRIT; see the video recording on this website:
(https://www.ted.com/talks/angela_lee_duckworth_the_key_to_success_grit#t-3029)
(Access date: 5 December, 2015)

to achieve success, and that this can be learnt through developing GRIT qualities, as well as developing a "growth mindset". These characteristics may be described as follows:

- A burning desire to contribute so you can make a difference, regardless of the field of interest.
- Perseverance; you have a long-term view with regard to what you are doing and you don't shy away from your goal.
- Moral courage; do not compromise the values you believe in.
- Self-discipline, stubbornness or tenacity; you don't give up although others choose something else.

The simple reason why managers should develop GRIT in their employees is the formula: GRIT= Success.

Seligman's formula for achievement may be expressed as: Achievement = skill x effort (Seligman, 2011:115). If we relate Seligman's formula for achievement to GRIT, we arrive at the following synthesis for personal success: GRIT multiplied by time and energy used on task (Personal success = GRIT x time used x energy).

The time required to be world class within a specific field is: "60 hours a week on it for ten years", says Seligman (2011:115). Thus, in practice, to become a global leader within a specific field requires roughly 31,000 hours within the specific area of work. To be an expert in a field one must work 10,000 hours says Seligman (2011: 115). Consequently, what distinguishes the expert from the prospective world leader is thus a much greater effort over a longer period of time. The research around GRIT has also shown the following relationship: "—older people have more GRIT than younger people--" (Seligman, 2011:122). This is important to take into consideration with regard to which co-workers managers should aim for, if business' performance is in focus, and not myths about people's performance.

The next section describes, analyses and discusses the next element in Fig. 2, adaptability and self-regulation.

Adaptability and self-regulation

According to Petterson (2012), positive psychology has been an academic field from the neck upwards ever since the field was developed. This has also been an objection to positive psychology (Anderson, 2001). Accordingly we attempt here, in discussing self-image in relation to positive psychology, to infer the significance of the body for the development and maintenance of the self-image (Hefferon, 2013). We do this because it seems reasonable to assume that self-image is affected by the physical body, as asserted by Demaree, et al., (2006).

We define self-regulation as having control of one's emotions, thoughts and behaviour

(Segerstrøm, et al., 2011:25). When an individual does not possess self-regulation, many problems may arise (Baumeister & Vohs, 2004). There is a strong correlation in the research between a negative self-image of one's own body and, eating disorders, alcoholism, depression, social anxiety, etc. (Swami, et al., 2010). The good news is that a positive body image, can be developed by various techniques, through, inter alia, the so-called PBI (positive body image) (Tylka, 2011).

Wellness, wellbeing and self-esteem are closely related to an individual's perception and notions about their own bodies writes Meier, et al., (2012: 707). Hefferon points out that the body thus becomes embedded in our overall self-image (2015: 791). She emphasises the following points with respect to the relationship between self-image and the body (2015:794):

- our perception of our own body
- our feelings about how our body appears
- how one experiences one's own body when moving among others
- how satisfied / dissatisfied one is with one's body or parts of it.

Self-regulation concerns both the physical body and our thoughts and actions. To achieve self-regulation requires our full attention. Both our thinking and our communication must be focused in order to prevent insulting or offending others. Self-regulation requires that we constantly focus on positive social interaction, although we may feel that it is the other party who bears responsibility for a tense situation. In other words, often the best way to change others is to change your reaction to their behaviour (Segerstrøm, et al., 2011:25). It is crucial to a positive outcome of social interaction that one continuously takes the perspective of others; this might also be designated Asplund's motivation theory. In brief, this concerns: *People are motivated by social response* (Asplund, 2010: 221-229).

One should be aware of the fact that the ability to self-regulate deteriorates after a situation where one really has put every effort into controlling oneself. That is, one becomes tired exerting all one's efforts on self-regulation in an initial situation, and when a new situation develops immediately after, the ability to self-regulate has been weakened. It may be said that the ego is weakened through using it to control certain behaviour; this is called ego depletion (Muraven & Baumeister, 2000). Figuratively, this may be compared to a muscle that gets tired after exertion; research suggests that one has a limited resource available regarding self-regulation. This resource may be understood in two ways. On the one hand, you become tired after using this resource, so that in the next task or situation your ability to self-regulate has been reduced. On the other hand, you also develop the resource by using it, not unlike what happens to muscles with increased use.

Some control strategies can alleviate the fatigue problems mentioned above. There are two particular strategies that are relatively simple that can be performed by the individual. The first strategy is attentional redeployment (Gross, 2001). In this strategy, one tries to focus attention on something positive, something you appreciate in the other / others. The second strategy is called cognitive reappraisal (Segerstrøm, et al., 2011:25). This involves being "present in the moment", and thinking positively about the other/ others and then acting on the basis of this new way of thinking (Langer,2011:279-293).

Poor self-regulation with respect to thought processes manifests itself as anxiety, brooding and intrusive thoughts that interfere with concentration (Segerstrøm, et al., 2011:30). Good self-regulation affects various bodily functions positively, such as blood glucose, cortisol levels, heart rate, etc. (Gailliot & Baumeister, 2007).

Regulation of emotions concerns how one can influence one's own emotions, and how they are experienced and expressed (Gross, 1998). Effective self-regulation of thoughts, feelings and behaviour can be seen in the context of wellness, well-being and the good life, better cognitive functions, less anxiety and brooding, more positive emotions and easier social interaction (Segerstrøm, et al., 2011: 33).

In the next section, we will describe, analyse and discuss the next element in Fig. 1, personal strength and powers of endurance.

Personal strength and powers of endurance

Working from one's strengths is something rather different from being rewarded because one performs a work task well. Research shows that only one in three people can explain what their strengths are (Linley, et al., 2010:65). Most people believe that their strengths are in the areas for which they are rewarded, and for which they receive positive feedback because of performing tasks well (Linley, et al., 2010:65). Personal strength is based on the burning desire of an individual to make a difference, and also the energy he/she invests in realizing that burning desire (Dweck, 2012; Seligman, 2011:102-125).

When developing strengths it may be ineffective strategy to identify where the employee is weak, and then improve these areas. A better strategy may be to identify where the employee has potential and then improve precisely these areas. The individual should develop his/her ability to discover where they have potential to be extremely good, and then improve and refine these areas of expertise. For the individual, this is related to the areas where he/she has a burning desire to make a difference that really makes a difference for themselves and/or others.

Through discussion with the employee, a manager can discover where he/she has a burning desire to make a difference. Subsequently, the employee can be allocated resources to develop this area of competence. Furthermore, the manager may improve organizational capabilities by identifying and improving the area of competence where the employee already has skills and ability. By taking this dual strategic approach, the organization has the opportunity to play among the global elite. These ideas are associated with the research of Dweck (2012) and Seligman (2006, 2011, 2013). However, if the manager attempts to improve employees in the areas they are not so good at, this will only raise the organization up to a mediocre level.

A Gallup survey posed the following question to 198,000 employees spread across large parts of the world: *At work, do you have the opportunity to do what you do best every day*. When responses were analysed it turned out that those organizations (and departments within organizations) that did best, were those where employees had the greatest opportunity to do what they were best at. The organizations that gave staff the opportunity to continually spend more of their time in areas they were really good at showed a strong increase in productivity (Buckingham & Clifton, 2005:3). The negative aspect shown by the Gallup survey was that most organizations do not give employees the opportunity to work on a daily basis with tasks where they can use their expertise. In other words, there seems to be a great potential for improvement in organisations regarding this area. In a large study where 1.7 million people in 63 countries were given the same question as above, it turned out that only 20 percent responded positively (Buckingham & Clifton, 2005:4). Thus, viewed from one perspective, it might be said that organizations are dumber than they need to be, because they only utilize 20 percent of their capability.

How should the individual be able to discover this strength, this hidden talent in themselves, and how should organizations utilize it? We answer this question by developing the following methodology associated with Buckingham & Clifton (2005):

1. Discover the deep desire in yourself, where you can make a difference.
2. Examine the pattern of your spontaneous reactions to an unforeseen act, event or reaction to a piece of news in the media. If you respond with a high degree of enthusiasm and

intensity, then there is a great probability that this is an area that may be defined as the one where you have a burning desire to make a difference.

3. Uncover the areas where your learning curve rises steepest. It is likely that this is an area that is connected to your burning desire.
4. Identify the areas that really satisfy your curiosity.

The four points above reveal how your burning desire may be aroused. This is where the individual has their basic potential. This also corresponds with Dweck's research (2012).

Strength and endurance grow when we focus on what we are good at, because this gives us energy. Therefore, our burning desire is our starting point. It may often be the case that we are not able to differentiate between the area where we have our qualifications and the area where our burning desire lies. The rationale is that we are rewarded for behaviour related to the area where we have received our training and education, and where we have good abilities, but this does not necessarily relate to where we have our burning desire. In other words, being paid a good salary for what we do is often misinterpreted as being synonymous with what we are passionate about. However, if we focus solely on this and not where we have our burning desire, then we risk becoming burnt out instead of getting energy and kindling the flame in ourselves and others.

The above discussion centres on reducing our learned behaviour, which we are rewarded for, and increasing the focus on our burning desire. This can develop personal strength that can contribute to individuals and organizations becoming world leaders within a specific area. In addition, we should opt out of the areas where our abilities are weak or poor. If we follow this strategy, then it is highly probable that we will develop our strength and endurance (Linley, et al., 2010).

In other words, we should continue to do what we are good at, but change our focus towards our burning desire. If we manage to connect the areas we are good at to what we are really passionate about, then we will have created an energy field that we can really take advantage of. This is where we will find our personal strength. The feeling that one experiences when one uses one's personal strength may almost be described by using Csikszentmihaly's (2002; 2013) concept of "flow". The people who experience flow vibrate with energy and excitement. They have reached into their burning desire, and experience a feeling that this is what they were born to do, say Linley, et al., (2010: 66). One of the consequences of coming into contact with and using their personal strength is that people feel better, are happier and perform at a higher level than those who do not use their personal strength.

The people who come into contact with their personal strength, through, for example, a flow situation, are subjected to a momentous experience. This experience gives the individual an opportunity for personal growth (Wethington, 2003:37-51). Such an experience changes many people's self-image, identity and even their faith in the meaning of life (Clausen, 1993). The consequences of such momentous experiences are not unlike Bateson's (1972) concept calibration. In calibration the individual undergoes a complete change in their character. His/her way of thinking and acting changes completely, due to such momentous experiences, points out Bateson. Momentous experiences, as they are used here, are thus the events that result in a person changing their thinking and behaviour radically.

Momentous experiences may be caused by several factors. Research shows that only about 10 percent experience momentous events through therapy (Wethington, 2003: 46). Most or about 75 percent report momentous experiences as a result of new challenges or disclosure of and insight into their own character flaws (Wethington, 2003: 46). The remaining part in the survey reported by Wethington refers to health problems and the insights these problems resulted in. Personal strength and endurance was reported as an important element that helped people through these momentous experiences.

In an organizational context, flow, momentous events and personal strength are on par with Linda Gratton's "Hot Spot" (2012), i.e., the areas in an organization that bubble with energy and innovative ideas. Metaphorically, this is people and teams who radiate and spread energy (Gratton, 2009). Managers must uncover these areas in teams and individuals. Thereafter, the focus should be on the burning desire of the teams and individuals, because it is here the potential to develop excellence lies.

Endurance may be described briefly as finishing something one has started up. This can be any project. Endurance shows itself when obstacles arise. One sticks to the task and finalizes what one has undertaken to complete. In practice, endurance is linked to a target. The person who perseveres completes the project and reaches the target, no matter how difficult it gets underway and no matter what obstacles and inconveniences he/she encounters.

Endurance is not something that is new in science; folk tales, sagas, myths and the literature of antiquity such as Homer and Sophocles provide countless examples. There were heroes who persevered and stood against evil forces. Evil could be disguised as a dragon, a hobgoblin, a Norwegian troll, an evil stepmother in fairy tales, etc.

In psychology research has been done on so-called "dandelion children", who despite their poor upbringing conditions have done very well. They are called "dandelion children" because they manage to thrive under any conditions much like the dandelions garden owners try to be rid of. These children are characterized by their perseverance, and research has failed to provide adequate explanations. The only thing that was revealed was that these children thrived despite an adverse upbringing that should have left them "stunted" (Masten, et al., 2011:117-119). Personal strength and endurance is for many people about succeeding, even where one would not have thought it possible.

Conclusion

In this chapter we have investigated the following issue: How can managers establish workplace conditions conducive to facilitating a sense of mastery for employees? During the course of this chapter we have made it clear that a sense of mastery promotes an individual's work performance.

There are three things that are apparent in the Gallup survey mentioned above. Effective managers focus on the personal strengths of their employees. Managers select and surround themselves with the right people. Successful managers see and understand employees' need to work on things that they are passionate about.

IQ tests are much used when psychologists and other researchers attempt to predict individuals' future performance. One point here is that these tests are very well tested and their comprehensive nature means that they can be used to measure many different factors. Our point is that only a few, if any of the qualities measured by the Grit scale, such as self discipline, for example, contribute to the result of an IQ test. If it is the case that self discipline and the other qualities measured by the Grit scale are really those that predict future success, then IQ tests are problematic, and should be complemented with Grit tests. According to Seligman (2011:116), tests for self-discipline are little developed. Such tests, among others, have been developed by Angela Lee Duckworth to remedy this deficiency.

Our answer to the issue discussed in this chapter is to develop a model that relates to the description, analysis and discussion in this chapter. The model can be applied by managers in order to develop employees' ability to feel a sense of mastery. Used in this way, the model functions also as a methodological and conceptual tool available for managers to use to develop the individual, the team and the organization in order to become world leaders. By focusing on an individual's ability to feel a sense of mastery, a manager can develop his/her organization into a world leader within the highly limited area where each and every employee has a burning desire to make a difference.

Fig. 3. How can managers promote mastery at the workplace?

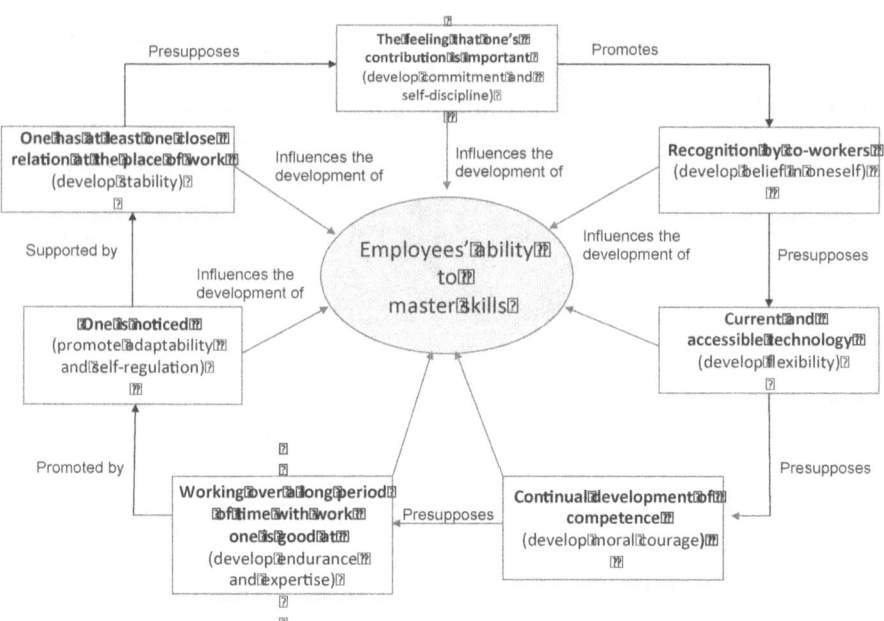

References

Asplund, J. (2010). Det sociala livets elementära former, Korpen, Stockholm

Asplund, J. & Blacksmith, N. (2013). Productivity through strengths, in Cameron, K.S. & Spreitzer, G.M. The Oxford Handbook of Positive Organizational Scholarship, Oxford University Press, Oxford. pp. 353-365.

Bandura, A. (1977). Self-efficacy: Towards a unifying theory of behavioral change, Psychological Review, 84:191.215.

Bandura, A. (2001). Social cognitive theory: An agentic perspective, Annual Review of Psychology, 52:1-26.

Bandura, A. (2006). Towards a psychology of human agency, Perspectives on Psychological Science, 1:164-180.

Bateson, G. (1972). Steps to an Ecology of Mind, Intex Books, New York.

Baumeister, R.F.; Campell, J.D.; Krueger, J.I. & Vohs, K.D. (2003). Does high self-esteem cause better performance, interpersonal success, happiness, or healthier lifestyles? Psychological Science in Public Interest, 4:1-44.

Baumeister, R.F. & Vohs, K.D. (2004). Handbook of self-regulation: Research, theory, and applications, Guilford, New York.

Bednar, R.; Wells, G. & Petterson, S. (1989). Self-esteem: Paradoxes and innovations in clinical theory and practice, American Psychological Association, Washington, DC.

Buckingham, M. & Clifton, D.O. (2005). Now discover your strengths: How to develop your talents and those of the people you manage, Pocket Books, London.

Carr, A. (2011). Positive Psychology, Routledge, London.

Clausen, J.A. (1993). American lives: Looking back at the children of the great depression, The Free Press, New York.

Cotman, C.W.; Berchtold, N.C. & Christie, L. (2007). Exercise builds brain health: Key roles of growth factor cascades and inflammation, Trends in Neurosciences, 30:464-472.

Csikszentmihaly, M. (2002). Flow: The Psychology of Happiness: The Classic Work on How to Achieve Happiness, Rider, New York.

Csikszentmihaly, M. (2013). Creativity: The Psychology of Discovery and Invention, Harper, New York.

Davidson, R.J.; Jackson, J.D. & Kalin, N.H. (2000). Emotion, plasticity, context, and regulation: Perspectives from affective neuroscience, Psychological Bulletin, 126:890-909.

Demaree, H.A.; Pu, J.; Robinson, J.; Schmeichel, B,J.; Everhart, E. (2006). Predicting facial valence to negative stimuli from resting RSA: Not a function of active emotion regulation, Cognition and Emotion, 20:161-176.

Durlak, J.A.; Weissberg, R.P. & Pachan, M. (2010). A meta-analysis of after-school programs that seek to promote personal and social skills in children and adolescents, American Journal of Community Psychology, 45,3/4:294-309.

Dutton, J.E.; Morgan Roberts, L. & Bednar, J. (2010). Pathways for positive identity construction at work: Four types of positive identity and the building of social resources, Academy of Management Review, 35:265-293.

Dutton, J.E.; Morgan Roberts, L. & Bednar, J. (2011). Prosocial practices, positive identity, and flourishing at work, i Donaldson, S.I.; Csikszentmihalyi, M. & Nakamura, J., Applied positive psychology, improving everyday life, health, schools, work, and society, Routledge, New York.

Dutton, J.E. & Roberts, L.M. (2009). Exploring positive identities and organizations: Building a theoretical and research foundation, Routledge, New York.

Dweck, C.S. (2012). Mindset, Robinson, New York.

Fredrickson, B. (2014). Positivity, Oneworld, New York.

Gailliot, M.T. & Baumeister, R.F. (2007). The physiology of willpower: Linking blood glucose to self-control, Personality and Social Psychology Review, 11:133-151.

Gratton, L. (2009). Glow, Financial Times/Prentice Hall, New York.

Gratton, L. (2012). Hot Spots: Hot Spots: Why Some Teams, Workplaces, and Organization Buzz With Energy-and Others Dont's, Read How You Want, London.

Greene, R. (2012). Mastery, Profile Books, New York.

Gross, J.J. (1998). The emerging field of emotion regulation: An integrative review, Review of General Psychology, 2:271-299.

Gross, J.J. (2001). Emotion regulation in adulthood: Timing is everything, Current Directions in Psychological Science, 10:214-219.

Haney, P. & Durlak, J.A (1998). Changing self-esteem in children and adolescents: A meta-analytic review, Journal of clinical child psychology, 27:423-433.

Hefferon, K. (2013). Positive psychology and the body: The somapsychic side of flourishing, McGraw-Hill, London.

Hefferon, K. (2015). The role of embodiment in optimal functioning, i Joseph, S. Positive psychology in practice, Wiley, London. S. 791-805.

Kempermann, G.H.; Kuhn, G. & Gage, F.H. (1997). More hippocampal neurons in adult mice living in an enriched environment, Nature, 86:493-495.

Langer, E. (2011). Mindfulness versus positive evaluation, in Lopez, S.H. & Snyder, C.R. The oxford handbook of positive psychology, Oxford

University Press, Oxford. pp. 279-293.

Linley, A.; Willars, J. & Biswas-Diener, R. (2010). The strengths book, CAPP Press, London.

Maddux, J. (2009). Self-efficacy: The power of believing you can. In Lopez, S. & Snyder, R. (ed.). Oxford Handbook of Positive Psychology, Oxford University Press, Oxford. pp. 335-344.

Maddux, J. & Winstead, B.A. (2015). Psychopathology: Foundations for a contemporary understanding, Routledge, Oxford.

Masten, A.S.; Cutuli, J.J.; Herbers, J.E. & Reed, M-G, J. (2011). Resilience in development, in Lopez, S.H. & Snyder, C.R. The oxford handbook of positive psychology, Oxford University Press, Oxford. pp. 117-131.

Meier, B.P.; Schnall, S.; Schwartz, N. & Bargh, J.A. (2012). Embodiment in social psychology, Topics in Cognitive Science, 4,4:705-716.

Morgan Roberts, L. & Creary, S.J. (2013). Positive Identity Construction, Insights from classical and contemporary theoretical perspectives, i Cameron, K.S. & Spreitzer, G.M., The Oxford Handbook of Positive Organizational Scholarship, Oxford University Press, Oxford.

Mruk, C. (1999). Self-esteem, Free Association Books, London. pp. 70-84.

Mruk, C. (2006). Self-esteem: Theory, research and practice, Springer, New York.

Muraven, M. & Baumeister, R.F. (2000). Self-regulation and depletion of limited resources: Does self-control resemble a muscle? Psychological Bulletin, 126:247-259.

Petterson, C. (2012). Pursuing the good life: 100 reflections on positive psychology, Oxford University Press, Oxford.

Petterson, C. & Park, N. (2011). Character strengths and virtues: Their role in well-being, in Donaldson, S.I.; Csikszentmihalyi, M. & Nakamura, J. Applied positive psychology, Routledge, London.

Robins, R.; Tracy, J. & Trzesniewski, K. (2008). Naturalising the self, in Oliver, J.P..; Robins, R. & Pervin, L. (ed.). Handbook of Personality: Theory and research, Guilford Press, New York. pp. 421-447.

Segerstrøm, S.C.; Smith, T.W. & Eisenlohr-Moul, T.A. (2011). Positive psychophysiology: The body and self regulation, in Sheldon, K.M.; Kashdan, T.B. & Steger, M.F., Designing positive psychology, Oxford University Press, Oxford. pp. 25-40.

Seligman, M.E. (2006). Learned optimism, Vintage Books, New York.

Seligman, M.E. (2011). Flourish, Nicolas Brearly Publishing, New York.

Seligman, M.E. (2013). What you can change, and what you can´t, Nicholas Brealey Publishing, New York.

Skager, R. & Kerst, E. (1989). Alcohol and drug use and self-esteem: A psychological perspective. In Mecca, A.M.; Smelser, N.J. & Vasconcellos, J. (ed.) The social importance of self-esteem, University of California Press, Berkeley. pp. 248-293.

Swami,V.; Begum, S. & Petrides, K.V. (2010). Associations between trait emotional intelligence, actual-ideal weight discrepancy, and positive body image, Personality and individual Differences, 49, 5:485-489.

Swann, W.; Chang-Schneider, C. & Larsen McClarty, K. (2007). Do people´s self-views matter? Self-concept and self-esteem in everyday life, American Psychologist, 62, 2:84-94.

TylkaT.L. (2011). Positive Psychology perspectives on body image, Body image: A handbook of science, practice and prevention, Guilford Press, New York.

Wethington, E. (2003). Turning points as opportunities for psychological growth, in Corey, L: ; Keyes, M. & Haidt, J. Flourishing: Positive Psychology and the life well- lived, American Psychological Association,

Washington, DC.

Chapter 5 Attitude change in Negotiations

Introduction

There is no consensus regarding how attitudes may be defined (Fabrigar, et al., 2005: 79). Baker, who takes a practical and realistic approach to understanding attitudes, says that they are constituted in relation to how we think, communicate and act (Baker, 1995: 154). She further explains that it is these three elements that should be considered when attempting to influence the changing of attitudes. This is also the structure we adopt in this chapter. The majority of definitions also consider evaluation: i.e. attitudes are evaluations in relation to something or someone along a scale from positive to negative (Fabrigar, et al., 2005: 79; Cooper, et al., 2016: 4-7). Further, attitudes are also directed at something or someone. Thurstone

(1946: 39) says that attitudes are "the intensity of positive or negative affect for or against a psychological object." Thus, the point here is that it would make little sense to denote an attitude by using a single index; this would be analogous to using a single numerical index in at attempt to describe an object such as a kitchen table say Fabrigar, et al., (2005: 79).

Attitude, as the concept is used here, includes a tendency to act in certain ways in relation to a psychological object, with which we associate certain positive or negative effects. Thus, the definition we use in the chapter may be summarized as follows: *Attitudes are defined as our way of thinking, communicating and acting (behaving) in relation to a psychological object, with which we associate certain positive or negative effects.* This definition is thus based on both Baker's and Thurston's definitions of attitudes. The definition consists primarily of three elements that work together to constitute and change attitudes: thinking, communication, and action (behaviour); another element, effects, are an intrinsic dimension of the other three elements. The definition we use does not say anything about an attitude's stability or possibility of change. However, the definition says something about some of the activities that create and change attitudes about people, psychological objects, problems and challenges.

How attitudes are formed seems to have a bearing on how stable they are (Cooper, et al., 2016:24). The constitution of attitudes may be divided into biological, social and experiential components (Tesser, 1993; Tesser & Martin, 1996). It seems reasonable to assume that attitudes that have a biological and evolutionary anchoring are harder to change than attitudes that are constituted through socialization processes. Moreover, it also seems reasonable to assume that attitudes that are constituted on the basis of an individual's experiences may be more easily changed than those that have roots in biological and socialization processes.

An attitude's stability is largely related to how it has been constituted, which is indicated by Cooper et al. (2016: 24). Although the influence of genetics on attitudes has been discussed by theorists, knowledge is uncertain in this area (Tesser, 1993). However Tesser & Martin (1996) say that genetic inheritance influences attitudes directly in the following cases:

1. When we are unable to relate an attitude to an empirical basis. For example, the new-born child's attitude to various facial expressions, such as the mother's.

2. When we cannot relate cultural influences to an attitude.

3. When the attitude relates to the theory of evolution. The new-born child's response to the mother's various facial expressions, say Cosmides et al. (1992), could indicate an evolutionary survival strategy where the child through evolutionary processes has

adapted to the facial expressions that have led to improved survival.

4. When the attitude is consistent with biological factors, as in the case of positive attitudes towards calorie-rich foods. The consumption of food that provided a surplus of carbohydrates and fat was important in pre-historic times because this offered a greater chance of survival. This is an example of an attitude that once had a clear function that continues to exist, although its function has become void in a different context.

Tesser (1993) and Tesser & Martin (1996) say indirectly that genes evolve and change through evolutionary processes. Although there are clear indications that biological factors play a role in relation to the constitution of certain attitudes, there is no unambiguous correlation say Yu & Sheppard (1998).

In several studies of twins, researchers have discovered a factor they call "inherited attitudes" whose relatively high probability (50 percent in some studies) makes it important (Tesser, 1993; Robertson & Cooper, 2011: 9-10). The biological make-up of an individual may provide him/her with certain advantages that others do not necessarily possess. An example of this might be dispositions that influence personality and abilities, which may be instrumental in the development of certain attitudes. In other words, research indicates the importance of biological factors with respect to the attitudes we develop, albeit indirectly.

Thus, some attitudes may be biologically determined, directly and indirectly, whereas other attitudes may be the result of social inheritance. Attitudes may also be acquired through an individual's experiences. However, it must be noted that although attitudes are developed through our experiences, there are also certain dispositions, both biological and cultural, that influence the attitudes an individual develops through their experiences (Zajonc, 1968; 2000; Banaji, et al., 2001). If one has personal experience of the attitude's object, then it is highly probable that the attitude becomes stable and durable (Regan & Fazzio, 1977).

Attitudes that are a product of biological inheritance, directly or indirectly, are more stable than attitudes that are socially acquired, and attitudes based on the individual's experiences. This may be understood as an attitude-hierarchy in relation to the degree of stability versus possibility of change. Another aspect is whether an attitude has a strong or weak positive valence relative to an object (Cooper, et al., 2016: 23). In other words, the weaker the valence, the easier it is to change an attitude, and vice versa. Valency is related to the engagement one has with a positive or negative object. It is also the case that an attitude with a strong valence is easier to recall from memory than an attitude with a low valence. A strong attitude also has greater influence on how we process information about the attitude's objects than a weak attitude (Holland, et al., 2002). This has implications for how resistant the individual is to being persuaded to change an attitude.

An attitude's stability versus its possibility of change is also related to the attitude's permeability in the individual's world. The stronger valence an attitude has towards an object, the greater the likelihood that other objects are considered in light of the strong attitude (Cooper, 2016: 23-24). The same applies to extreme attitudes (Bassili, 2008). Another insight regarding extreme attitudes is that the more extreme an attitude is, the greater the likelihood that the individual acts on the basis of this attitude (Peterson & Dutton, 1975). In addition, extreme attitudes often result in the individual being the victim of a false consensus effect. This effect makes the individual think that more people are in agreement than is actually the case (Allison & Meesik, 1988).

In the following, we structure stability of attitude versus change of attitude in relation to the definition established in the introduction. This definition consists of three main elements: thinking, communication and behaviour.

The **problem approach we are investigating is the following**: How can managers change the attitudes of their employees?

We have developed three research questions on the basis of our definition of attitude:

Research question 1: How can managers change employees' attitudes through the way they think?

Research question 2: How can managers change employees' attitudes through the way they communicate?

Research question 3: How can managers change employees' attitudes through behaviour?

The introduction, problem approach and research questions are summarized in the model in Figure 1, which also shows how the chapter is organized.

Figure 1. Structuring of attitudes: A systemic model

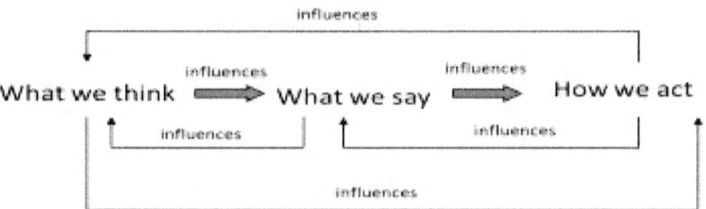

How attitudes change through how we think

The question we examine in this section is: How can managers change employees' attitudes through the way they think?

Our way of thinking is closely related to our "belief system" (Wyer & Albarracin, 2005: 273-322; Fishbein, 2008: 137-142), and our information processes (Wegner & Carlson, 2005: 498-499). Our "belief system" may be understood as a coherent system of assumptions and perceptions. This "belief system" comes into play when we evaluate something or someone (Eagly & Chaiken, 1998). The system of assumptions and beliefs is constituted in part by a lack of reliable information (Eagly & Chaiken, 1993: 257-305; Wyer & Albarracin, 2005: 273).

The perception the individual has of an object also affects his/her actions regarding the object (Fishbein, 2008: 137). Fishbein points out that although the individual may have various perceptions of an object, it is his/her final evaluation that represents their attitude. This attitude will also very likely emerge in future meetings with the object (Fishbein, 2008: 137).

Perceptions that are based on one's own experiences are often considered as if they are factual knowledge in memory (Wyer, 2004). In this way, experience-based information about a psychological object is often interpreted as a "truth" (Wyer & Albarracin, 2005: 274). When we convey this information further or use the information when making a decision, it is often considered "fact" (Schwarz & Bohner, 2001). Experiential knowledge has a high degree of influence, according to Wyer & Albarracin (2005: 281) when it:

1. Has been newly acquired

2. Has been used in practical situations earlier

3. Is used often

4. Is associated with other knowledge that supports the experiential knowledge

5. Is related to general knowledge ideas about the object

As early as 1935, Allport noted that attitudes determine what we "see" and what we "hear" (Allport, 1935: 806). This underlines the importance of attitudes with respect to information and knowledge processes. Although Allport's perspective has been criticized by many scientists over the years, most agree that there is a strong relationship between attitudes and the way we process information regarding an object (Wegner & Carlston, 2005: 498-499). This is especially the case if an attitude is related to fact-based knowledge (Wood, et al., 1985).

The attitudes we have already activated will also affect the information we seek and how we evaluate it (Fabrigar, et al., 2005: 101). Much empirical research suggests that the acceptance of new information is influenced by attitudes we already possess.

New information is often shown to be distorted in relation to the motivation one has in the collection of data (Marsh & Wallace, 2005: 376-377). One might say that this helps to reinforce the resistance to change in the cognitive system, or as Abelson (1986) puts it: one treats one's attitudes as one's own property, and protects them in the best possible way.

The attitude one has before an event, situation or action affects our evaluation of the end result. One could say that we tend to consider "facts" through our "coloured glasses", or that our subjective evaluation prevails in relation to objective facts. Similarly, Marsh & Wallace (2005: 376-379), say that our evaluations are motivated by our "belief system".

The following measures that can be implemented by managers may be inferred from the above description and analysis.

Manager-measure 1: Managers who take employees' experiences into consideration may contribute to changing employees' attitudes.

Manager-measure 2: Managers who use factual knowledge contribute to changing attitudes among employees.

How attitudes change through what we say

The question we examine in this section is: How can managers change employees' attitudes through the way they communicate?

Information's cognitive authority is the term we use here to describe, analyse and discuss changes in attitudes related to how we communicate when trying to influence attitudes. Wilson (1983: 13) emphasizes that information's cognitive authority is connected to a relationship between two people, and that cognitive authority will vary. Further, he emphasizes that cognitive authority is related to areas of interest, and he discusses why we tend to believe more in one type of information than in another.

The fact that we believe in one type of information in preference to another, and that we manage to convince others to believe in the information is directly linked to how we communicate to influence others. Lasswell (1948: 37) was the first who asked why we believe more in one type of information than another from a social-psychological perspective. He asked the following: Who says what to whom, through which channels, and with what effect? If we divide the question into several sub-questions then the following elements emerge:

- The sender of a message
- The message
- The media being used
- The receiver of the message

The sender has certain personal characteristics that influence us, and **the message** also has certain characteristics that affect us. The **receiver of the information** ascribes both the sender and message with certain characteristics.

In the following, we will structure the description, analysis and discussion in relation to the sender, message and receiver. We choose not to focus on how the choice of channels may affect the information's cognitive authority.

The sender

Why do we have more confidence in what one person says, than that of another?

Several studies report that our confidence in the information communicated by someone is determined by their appearance (Dermer & Thiel, 1975, Dion et al., 1972, Rucker et. al., 1981). However, it must be emphasized that the results are not entirely clear. We also have a negative bias towards people who are physically attractive. This applies to both men and women (Kleinke & Staneski, 1980; Hatfield & Sprecher, 1986)

The courtroom provides an example of a situation in which our credibility certainly is at stake. However, even here, where one would presume that law and justice prevailed, research has shown that a person's appearance, dress and behaviour are important and can affect the outcome of a case. This has been thoroughly documented by Hatfield & Sprecher (1986), among others.

An important point here is not only how the other presents himself/herself, but how we feel we present ourselves in relation to the other (Ross & Salvia,1975). Self-understanding and status act upon each other. By self-understanding we mean how we perceive ourselves in relation to others. By status we mean how the other perceives us. If a person signalises that he/she is above an assumed average in a situation, then the person's information will have less cognitive authority than if he/she signals that he/she is at an average level compared to colleagues (Hatfield & Sprecter, 1986). This may seem paradoxical. Although we may have confidence in the people who are themselves, we would not have full confidence in them if they were themselves but appeared to be above us. This can be explained by the fact that we have a built-in aversion to arrogance and condescension.

Manager-measure 3: The manager can change employees' attitudes by presenting themselves as being on the same level as the employees.

The message

The message is the smallest unit in a communication process. We choose to divide the message into two parts (Bateson, 1972; Luhmann, 1989)

1. The informational part
2. The communicative part

The informational part relates to what is said. The communicative part is how we say it. An essential part of changing attitudes is oriented around information exchange. However, we have a tendency to overestimate information that supports our attitudes and assumptions, and underestimate information that opposes them (Raifa, 1982: 338). We rarely actively seek information that goes against our existing beliefs or attitudes; we find support for this view in Pruitt & Carnevale (1993: 84) and Grzelak (1982). The fact that we tend to search for information that supports our established attitudes, instead of searching for information that could change our perceptions is also an important point made by Wason (1960, 1968; 1968a), Frey (1986) and Marsh & Wallace (2005:377). We also seek to avoid situations where our views may be exposed to pressure to change. In this way, the information process is affected by our motives when collecting information.

Information that goes against our beliefs has little cognitive authority. We find partial support for this statement in Bazerman (1994), Thompson (1991), Zubek et al. (1992). We give priority to what we already know, and thus we also economize our information processes, although this may lead in many cases to systematic fallacies (Fisher et al., 1991, Lax & Sebenius, 1986: 31). Perhaps the most provocative results regarding this phenomenon can be found in Tversky and Kahneman's work on prospect theory (1971; 1973; 1974; 1983; Kahneman, 2011).

Information, say Nisbet and Ross (1980: 45-51), stimulates and holds our attention when it:

1. Appears emotionally interesting.
2. Is specific and provocative.
3. Is close to us in time and space.

It is reasonable to assume that a link between the three types of information will have a greater effect than if there is only a single link. Furthermore, it is reasonable to assume that the longer we manage to direct people's attention to the information we present, and especially the three types of information, the greater cognitive authority the information will have, and the greater the likelihood that we can change people's attitudes. This is consistent with Tesser (1978) who explains this phenomenon by the fact that the memory thus becomes more active. It must also be emphasized that it is not only accurate information that has this effect on us. Misinformation, which is linked to the emotions, the specific and that which is close must be assumed to have as much impact, and we will find it difficult to protect ourselves against both the information-presentation and our own reactions to it.

Manager-measure 4: Managers who *use information related to emotions, the specific and that which is close* can contribute to changing employees' attitudes.

The receiver

The *expectations* we have of a person will affect how we react to their behaviour. If we trust them, then our behaviour towards them will reinforce this impression. However, if a different impression is created of the person, through rumours, gossip, or the like, then our behaviour towards them will also be different. Consequently, our attitude toward the person concerned will reinforce the behaviour we expect of them.

Manager-measure 5: The manager's *expectations* contribute to changing attitudes among the employees.

Thus, we gain confirmation of what we had expected to know beforehand. This applies even when there is no truth value in the expectations we have. This phenomenon in human interaction was first pointed out by Kelly (1950). Thus, attitudes towards another person have a force in themselves.

According to the expectancy-value model of Fischbein & Ajzen (1975), we ascribe the reference object a certain expected subjective probability so that the expectation occurs. A reference object is the object to which the information relates to. We also attribute characteristics to the reference object, i.e. specific values, positive or negative. Our attitude to the reference object is then the sum of our expectations multiplied by the values we attribute to it (attitude = sum of expectations * value).

It is reasonable to assume that information that supports our attitudes concerning the reference object will have greater cognitive authority than information that goes against our attitudes. We find support for this view in Sheppard, Hartwich & Warshaw (1988). Thus, information that supports our attitudes and beliefs would seem to have greater cognitive authority than information that goes against our attitudes and beliefs.

An essential point in the relationship between attitudes to the reference object and reliance in the information regarding the object is that the two elements can vary independent of each other. The attitude will vary in different contexts and at different times, but reliance on the information regarding the reference object will still be constant.

Our attitudes towards other people sometimes hinder the other person from communicating in a situation. We use past experience of similar types, and then we judge the person concerned on the basis of our own typology. In other words, there are other people that we've had some experience of, which determine how we behave towards the person we possibly know nothing of. Once a person has been registered in our type-registry, he/she is pigeon-holed, i.e. we have had experience before with "his/her type".

The result is that our type-registry creates a picture of the person from the type-registry. If the person behaves differently than our typology would suggest, then we react with anxiety, uncertainty and express a negative behaviour towards the person says Garfinkel (1967: 42-44).

Manager-measure 6: Managers who *take into consideration employees' typologies* will contribute to changing employees' attitudes in the desired direction.

How attitudes change through what we do

We will examine the following question: How can managers change employees' attitudes through behaviour?

Attitudes influence behaviour, but behaviour also influences attitudes (Fazio, 1986). We will describe, analyse and discuss this systematic relationship.

The relationship: Attitudes-behaviour

Can attitudes predict behaviour? The interesting issue related to the question is that people who demonstrate the same attitudes may have a high degree of variation in their behaviour.

It seems probable that people who are neo-liberalists would support free competition with an absence of monopoly and other factors restricting competition. However, is the relationship between attitudes and behaviour so simple? Research shows that a more pertinent question is: Under which conditions can attitudes predict behaviour? Early research on the subject (Wicker, 1969: 75) has shown that attitudes only predict two percent of variation in behaviour. Later research by Kraus (1995), in a larger meta-analysis of empirical research, found that the correlation was 38 percent. Regardless of whether one can explain the differences in various ways, for example, by use of methods, etc., the fact remains that there is no simple relationship between attitudes and behaviour. There is much research that suggests that the relationship is stronger under some conditions than others. We will investigate and systematize some of these conditions here. The relationship between attitudes and behaviour will always be influenced by issues of measurement. We refer readers to Maio & Haddock (2015:68-72) who discuss in detail issues related to choice of methods. In this systematization, we will not concern ourselves with how the choice of measurement indicators affect the outcome. We will also limit ourselves to attitudes that are related to behaviour, and not choose attitudes related to physical objects, such as the Eiffel Tower, Big Ben, the Twin Towers, the Statue of Liberty, the Little Mermaid, etc.

We will examine the following two categories of condition: situational conditions and personality conditions. We will further divide these condition categories into different types of conditions.

Condition category I: Situational conditions

We will examine two types of conditions here. We term one main type, theme, and the other context.

Condition 1: Theme

Research has shown that the theme one investigates will affect the outcome of how much one can rely on whether an attitude will predict behaviour. It is when one relates theme to a person's values that one can infer something about the prediction strength of an attitude, because the value hierarchy may be related to an attitude's strength (Effron & Miller, 2012; Eagly et al., 1999). Empirical research confirms that the stronger an attitude is, the greater the likelihood that the attitude will predict behaviour, and vice versa (Maio & Haddock, 2015:154-179; Cooke & Sheeran, 2004). One can imagine that one's values can be structured in a hierarchy of values; those that are lower in the hierarchy are not that important to the person, while those at the top of the hierarchy are extremely important.

The attitude towards a political candidate and the likelihood of voting for this candidate are relatively great (Kraus, 1995); empirical measurements have shown that the strength of this relationship attitude-behaviour (voting for political candidates) ranges between 63-78 percent, which is very high (Fazio & Williams, 1986). This may indicate that ideology lies high up in the value hierarchy.

Manager-measure 7: Managers who take into account *the strong attitudes of employees* will contribute to changing the attitudes of employees in the desired direction.

Condition 2: Context

The context an attitude is played out in has importance to what extent we can predict behaviour. If the context is related to social pressure, then it is highly probable that there will be consistency between attitudes and behaviour (Maio & Haddock, 2015:82-83).

If we expect our behaviour will get the desired result, then it is likely that our attitude corresponds to our behaviour. If we do not see any connection between attitude and behaviour, then it is less likely that our attitude predicts our behaviour. For example, if we see that the plastic waste we collect helps the environment, then the probability is great that our attitude towards a better environment will lead to positive actions towards the environment (Ajzen, 1991).

Manager-measure 8 : Managers who use *social pressure* from other employees in an organisation to change the attitude of the employee in focus will contribute to changing the employee's attitude in the desired direction.

Condition category II: Personality conditions

In addition to situational conditions an individual's personality is also of importance. We will examine two condition types: self-correction and time for reflection.

Condition 1: Self-correction

Empirical research shows that the attitudes of people who largely modify their behaviour in relation to the context and circumstances (high degree of adaption) have low prediction value of their behaviour. Those persons who do not modify their behavior in relation to the context and circumstances (low degree of adaption) are highly predictable regarding their behaviour (Snyder & Kendzierski, 1982).

Manager-measure 9: Managers base their efforts on employees who are flexible (high degree of adaptability) because these more easily will be able to change attitudes, and may be used later to exert social pressure on other employees.

Condition 2: The need for reflection time

Another personality condition that has proved to be important for an attitude's prediction value regarding behaviour is the need for reflection time. It has been shown that those people who have a great need for reflection time before they act have a strong correlation between attitude and action (Cacioppo & Petty, 1982). The explanation seems obvious. Those who have a great need for reflection are most likely thoughtful and reflective about their attitudes. The people who need reflection time before they act also spend more time thinking through the consequences of their actions.

Manager-measure 10: In a campaign aimed at changing attitudes managers should limit employees' time for reflection.

The relationship: Behaviour—attitudes

It is not only the case that behaviour can affect attitudes that is of interest, but also that behaviour does not need to conform to the attitudes we have. An important point is that people's attitudes can be changed by putting constraints on their behaviour. We will examine the following three conditions.

Condition 1: Social response

Asplund's motivation theory (Asplund, 1970; 2010) may be briefly summarized as: *People are motivated by social responses* (Asplund, 2010: 221-229). The following may be said to be central to Asplund's theory: *When people receive social responses, their level of activity increases.*

Manager-measure 11: Managers should provide positive social response in the direction they wish to change employees' attitudes.

Condition 2: The institutional framework

Asplund's motivation theory is consistent with North's action theory. North's theory may be expressed in the following statement: *People act on the basis of a system of rewards as expressed in the norms, values, rules and attitudes in the culture (the institutional framework)* (North, 1990; 1993;1994; 1996; 1997).

Manager-measure 12 : Managers should reward desired changes in attitude.

Condition 3: Social comparisons

In addition to Asplund and North, Festinger, before he developed the theory of cognitive dissonance (Festinger, 1957), developed a theory that people's behaviour is to a certain extent controlled by comparisons with others' attitudes (Festinger, 1954).

Manager-measure 13: Managers should get employees to compare themselves with groups who have the desired attitudes.

Conclusion

The problem we have examined in this chapter has been:

How can **managers** change **the attitudes of employees?**

We first examined how attitudes are constituted. This process may be divided into three parts. Firstly, there are attitudes that may be said to be biologically related. In practice, managers can do little to influence this type of attitude. Secondly, there are attitudes that are formed through socialization. This type of attitude is also difficult for management to change. Thirdly, there are attitudes that are constituted through an individual's own experiences. In this case, management has the possibility of influencing this type of attitude. What needs to be done is to first uncover the individual's attitude hierarchy. It may be imagined that the attitude hierarchy consists of attitudes of different strength and intensity. Those attitudes at the top of the attitude hierarchy have the greatest strength and intensity, while those at the bottom the least. The greater the strength and intensity an attitude has, the greater the likelihood is that managers **cannot** change the employee's attitude; the less the strength and intensity, the greater the likelihood a manager can change the employee's attitude. It is therefore critical that managers become aware of the individual's attitude hierarchy.

Managers can also utilise the structuring of attitudes, as discussed in the chapter, when attempting to influence employees' attitudes. In this context, three categories may be used: thinking, communication and behaviour.

For the category, **thinking**, managers must first deal with the employee's "belief system". To do this, it should be established to what extent the attitude is related to factual knowledge. Two strategies managers can use have been developed in the chapter in relation to the category thinking.

The category **communication** was divided into sender, message and receiver. To tackle change of attitudes in this category, managers can analyse and use how the employee presents himself/herself, what he/she says, how they say it, and what expectations the employee has. In the chapter, we developed four strategies for the category communication.

In the chapter, the category **behaviour** was divided into two types. The first type concerns how attitudes can predict behaviour. The second type is how behaviour can affect attitudes. The first type was divided into two conditions, situational conditions and personality conditions. In the chapter, we divided situational conditions into theme and context. In order to deal with "theme", it is crucial that the manager is able to discover the strength and intensity of the attitude (attitude hierarchy) that is connected to the actual theme. We have chosen to divide personality conditions into self-correction and time for reflection. Three manager strategies have been developed regarding the two personality conditions.

How behaviour can affect attitudes has been divided into three conditions. These are social response, the institutional framework's reward system and comparison with others. Three manager strategies have been developed regarding this category.

The discussion and analysis has been represented in an analytical model, which is a revised representation of Figure 1.

Figure 2. Analytical model: Changing attitudes

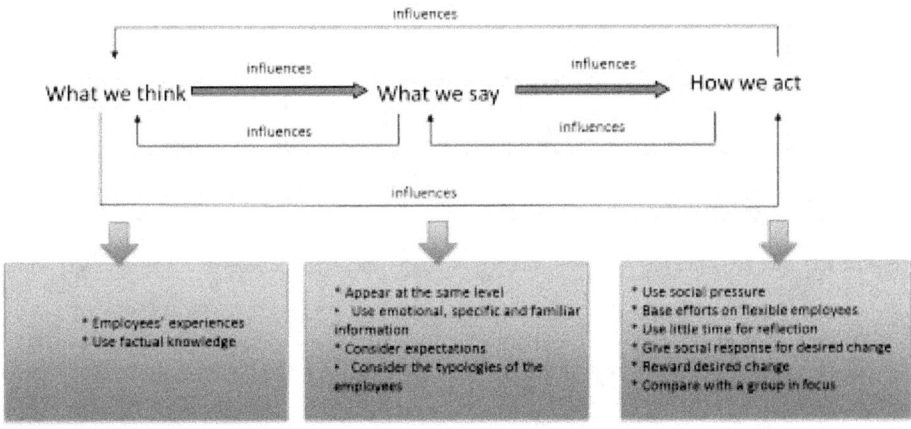

References

Abelson,, R.P. (1986). Beliefs are like possessions, Journal for the theory of social behaviour, 16: 223-250.

Allison, S.T. & Messick, D.M. (1988). The feature-positive effect, attitude strength, and degree of perceived consensus, Personality and Social Psychology Bulletin, 14, 2: 231-241.

Allport, G.W. (1935). Attitudes, in Murchison, C. (Ed.). Handbook of social psychology, Clark University Press, Worcester, MA. S. 798-844.

Asplund, J. (1970). Om undran innför samhället, Argos, Stockholm.

Asplund, J. (2010). Det sociala livets elementära former, Korpen, Stockholm

Bajani, M.R.; Lemm, K.M. & Carpenter, S.J. (2001). The social unconscious. In Tesser, A. & Schwarz (Ed.). Blackwell Handbook of social psychology, vol. 1. Intra-individual processes, Blackwell, Oxford. pp. 134-158.

Baker, R. (1995). Explaining attitudes, Cambridge University Press, Cambridge.

Bassili, J.N. (2008). Attitude strength, in Crano, W. D. & Prislin, R.

(Eds.). Attitude and Attitude Change, Psychology Press, pp. 237-261.

Bateson, G. (1972). Steps to an Ecology of Mind. Intex Books, London.

Bazerman, M.H. (1994). Judgement in Managerial Decision Making. John Wiley, New York.

Cacioppo, J.T. & Petty, R.E. (1982). The need for cognition, Journal of Personality and Social Psychology, 42: 116-131.

Cooke, R. & Sheeran, P. (2004). Moderation of cognition-intention and cognition-behaviour relations: A meta-analysis of properties of variables from the theory of planned behaviour, British Journal of Social Psychology, 43: 159-186.

Cooper, J.; Blackman, S.F. & Keller, K.T. (2016). The Science of Attitudes, Routledge, London.

Cosmides, L.; Tooby, J. & Barkow, J.H. (1992). Evolutionary psychology and conceptual integration, in Barkow, J.H.; Cosmides, L. & Tooby, J (eds.). The adapted mind: Evolutionary psychology and the generation of culture, Oxford University Press, Oxford. pp. 3-15.

Dermer, M. and D.L. Thiel (1975). When beauty may fail, Journal of

Personality and Social Psychology, 31: 1168-1176.

Dion, K., E. Berscheid and E. Hatfield (1972). What is beautiful is good, Journal of Personality and Social Psychology, 24: 285-290.

Eagly, A.H. & Chaiken, S. (1993). The Psychology of Attitudes, HBJ, New York. pp. 257-305.

Eagly, A.H. & Chen, S.; Chaiken, S. & Shaw-Barnes, K. (1999). The impact of attitude on memory: An affair to remember, Psychological Bulletin, 125:64-89.

Eagly, A.H. & Chaiken, S. (1998). Attitude structure and function, in Gilbert, D.T. & Fiske, S.T. (eds.). Handbook of social psychology, 4th. ed., Vol. 1, McGraw-Hill, Boston. pp. 269-322.

Effron, D.A. & Miller, D.T. (2012). How the moralization of issues grants social legitimacy to act on one's attitudes, Personality and Social Psychology Bulletin, 38:690-701.

Fabrigar, L.R.; MacDonald, T.K. & Wegener, D.T. (2005). The structure of attitudes, in Albarracin, D.; Johnson, B.T. & Zanna, M.P. The Handbook of Attitudes, Psychology Press, New York. pp. 79-124.

Fazio, R.H. (1986). How do attitudes guide behavior, Handbook of motivation and cognition: Foundations of Social Behavior. pp. 204.243.

Fazio R.H. & Petty, R.E. (2008). Conceptualizing attitudes, in Fazio R.H. & Petty, R.E. (Ed.) Attitudes: Their structure, function and consequences, Psychology Press, New York. pp. 1-5.

Fazio R.H. & Williams, C.J. (1986). Attitude accessibility as a moderator of attitude-perception and attitude-behavior relations: An investigation of the 1984 presidential election, Journal of Personality and Social Psychology, 51: 505-514.

Festinger, L. (1954). A theory of social comparison processes, Human Relations, 7, 2:117-140.

Festinger, L. (1957). A theory of cognition, Row Petterson, Evanston, IL.

Fishbein, M. (2008). An investigation of the relationship between beliefs about an object and the attitude toward that object, in Fazio, R.H. & Petty, R.E. (eds.). Attitudes, their structure, function and consequences, Psychology Press, New York. pp. 137-142.

Fishbein, M. and I. Ajzen (1975). Belief, attitude, intention and behavior: An introduction to theory and research. Addison-Wesley, Reading, M.A.

Fisher, R., W. Ury and B. Patton (1991). Getting to Yes. Business

Books, London.

Frey, D. (1986). Recent research on selective exposure to information, i Berkowitz, L. (Ed.). Advances in experimental social psychology, Academic Press, San Diego, CA. Vol. 19. pp. 41-80.

Garfinkel, H. (1967). Studies in Ethnomethodology. Polity Press, New York.

Grzelak, J.L. (1982). Preferences and cognitive processes in interdependence situations: A theoretical analysis of cooperation. In, V.J. Derlega and J. Grzelak (eds.), Cooperation and helping behavior: Theories and research (95-122). Academic Press, New York.

Hatfield, E. and S. Sprecher (1986). The Importance of Looks in Everyday Life: Mirror, Mirror. State University of New York Press, New York

Holland, R.W.; Verplanken, B. & Van Knippenberg, A. (2002). On the nature off attitude-behavior relations: The strong guide, the weak follow, European Journal of Social Psychology, 32,6:869-876.

Kahneman, D. (2011). Thinking fast and slow, Allen Lane, New York.

Kelley, H.H. (1950). The warm-cold variable in first impressions of persons, Journal of Personality, 18: 431-439.

Kleinke, C. L. and R.A. Staneski (1980). First impressions of female bust size, Journal of Social Psychology, 110: 123-134.

Kraus, S. (1995). Attitudes and the prediction of behavior: A meta-analysis of the empirical literature, Personality and social psychology bulletin, 21:58-75.

Lasswell, H.D. (1948). The Structure and Function of Communication in Society. In L. Bryson (Ed.). The Communication of Ideas: Religion and civilization series (37-51). Harper & Row, New York.

Lax, D.A. and J.K. Sebenius (1986). The Manager as Negotiator. Free Press, London.

Luhmann, N. (1989). Ecological communication, University of Chicago Press, Chicago.

Maio, G.R. & Haddock, G. (2015). Attitude change, in Kruglanski, A.W. & Higgins, E.T. (eds.). Social Psychology, Guilford Press, New York.

Marsh, K.L. & Wallace, H.M. (2005). The influence of attitudes on beliefs: Formation and change, , in Albarracin, D.; Johnson, B.T. & Zanna, M.P. (eds.). The Handbook of Attitudes, Psychology Press, New York. pp. 369-396..

Nisbett, R.E. and L. Ross (1980). Human inference: Strategies and shortcomings of social judgement. Prentice Hall, Englewood Cliffs, N.J.

North, D.C. (1990). Institutions, Institutional Change and economic performance, Cambrifge University Press, Cambridge.

North, D. (1993). Nobel lecture: http://www.nobelprize.org/nobel_prizes/economics/laureates/1993/north-lecture.html#not2, lesedato, 4.5.2012.

North, D.C. (1994). Economic performance through time, American Economic Review, 84: 359-368.

North, D.C. (1996). Epilogue: Economic performance through time. In Alston, L.J.; Eggertson, T. & North, D.C. "Empirical studies in institutional change", Cambridge University Press, Cambridge (pp. 342-355).

North, D.C. (1997). Prologue, 3-13 in J.N. Drobak & J.V.C. The frontiers of the new institutional economics, Academic Press, New York

Petersen, K.K. & Dutton, J.E. (1975). Centrality, extremity, intensity: Neglected variables in research on attitude behavior consistency, Social Forces, 54, 2:393-414.

Pruitt, D.G. and P.J. Carnevale (1993). Negotiation in social conflict. Open University Press, Buckingham.

Raiffa, H. (1982). The Art and Science of Negotiation. Harvard University Press, Cambridge, Mass.

Regan, D,T. & Fazzio, R. (1977). On the consistency between attitudes and behavior: Look to the method of attitude formation, Journal of Experimental Social Psychology, 13, 1:28-45.

Robertson, I. & Cooper, C. (2011). Well-Being: Productivity and happiness at work, Palgrace Macmillan, London.

Ross, M.B. and J. Salvia (1975). Attractiveness as a biasing factor in teaching judgments, American Journal of Mental Deficiency, 80: 96-98.

Rucker, M., D. Taber and A. Harrison (1981). The effect of clothing variation and first impressions of female job applicants; what to wear when, Social Behavior and Personality, 9: 53-64.

Schwarz, N. & Bohner, G. (2001). The construction of attitudes, in Tesser, A. & Schwarz, N. (eds.). Blackwell handbook of social psychology, intra-individual processes, vol. 1, Blackwell, Oxford, pp. 413-436.

Sheppard, B.H., J. Hartwick and P.R. Warshaw (1988). The Theory of Reasoned Action: A meta-Analysis of Past Research With Recommendations for Modifications and Future Research, Journal of Consumer Research, 15: 325-343.

Snyder, M, & Kendzierski, D. (1982). Acting on one´s attitudes: Procedures for linking attitudes and behavior, Journal of experimental Social Psychology, 18:165-183.

Tesser, A. (1978). Self-generated attitude change. In L. Berkowitz (Ed.). Advances in Experimental Social Psychology, Vol. 11. Academic Press, New York.

Tesser, A. (1993). The importance of heritability in psychological research: The case of attitude, Psychological Review, 100:129-142.

Tesser, A. & Martin, L.L. (1996). The psychology of evaluation. In Higgins, E.T. & Kruglanski, A.W. (Eds.). Social Psychology: Handbook of basic principles, Guilford, New York. pp. 400-432.

Thompson, L.L. (1991). Information exchange in negotiation, Journal of experimental Social Psychology, 27: 161-179.

Thurstone, L.L. (1946). Comment, American Journal of Sociology, 52:39-50.

Tversky, A. and D. Kahneman (1971). The belief in the law of numbers. Psychological Bulletin, 76: 105-110.

Tversky, A. & Kahneman, D. (1973). Availability: A heuristic for judging frequency and probability, Cognitive Psychology, 5: 207-232.

Tversky, A. and D. Kahneman (1974). Judgement under uncertainty: Heuristics and biases, Science, 185: 1124-1131.

Tversky, A. and D. Kahneman (1983). Extensional versus intuitive reasoning: The conjunction fallacy in probability judgment, Psychological Review,

Yu, D.W. & Sheppard, G.H. (1998). Is beauty in the eye of the beholder? Nature, 396: 321-322.

Wason, P.C. (1960). On the failure to eliminate hypotheses in a conceptual task, Quarterly Journal of Experimental Psychology, 12: 129-140.

Wason, P.C. (1968). Reason about a rule, Quarterly Journal of Experimental Psychology, 20: 273-283.

Wason, P.C. (1968a). On the failure to eliminate hypothesis: A second look. In P.C. Wason and P.N. Johnson Laird (eds.). Thinking and Reasoning. Penguin, Harmondsworth.

Wegener, D.T. & Carlston, D.E. (2005). Cognitive processes in attitude formation and change, in Albarracin, D.; Johnson, B.T. & Zanna, M.P. (eds.). The Handbook of Attitudes, Psychology Press, New York. pp. 493-542.

Wicker, A.W. (1969). Attitude versus actions: The relationship of verbal and overt behavioral responses to attitude objects, Journal of social issues, 25:41-78.

Wilson, P. (1983). Second-Hand Knowledge: An Inquiry into cognitive Authority. Greenwood Press, New York.

Wood, W.; Kallgren, C.A. & Preisler, R.M. (1985). Access to attitude relevant information in memory as a determinant of persuasion: The role of message attributes, Journal of Experimental Social Psychology, 21:73-85.

Wyer, R.S. (2004). Social comprehension and judgment: The role of situational models, narratives, and implicit theories, Erlbaum, Mahwah, NJ.

Wyer, R.S. & Albarracin, D. (2005). Belief formation, organization and change: Cognitive and motivational influence, in Albarracin, D.; Johnson, B.T. & Zanna, M.P. (eds.). The Handbook of Attitudes, Psychology Press, New York. pp. 273-322.

Zajonc, R.B. (1968). Attitudinal effects of more exposure, Journal of Personality and Social Psychology Monograph, 9, 2:1-27.

Zajonc, R.B. (2000). Feeling and thinking: Closing the debate over the independence of affect, In Forgas, J.P. (Ed.). Feeling and thinking: The role of affect in social cognition, Cambridge University Press, Cambridge.

pp. 31-58.

Zajonc, R.B. (2008). Feeling and thinking: Preferences need no inferences, in Fazio, R.H. & Petty, R.E. (eds.). Attitudes, their structure, function and consequences, Psychology Press, New York. pp. 143-168.

Zubek, J.M., D.G. Pruitt, R.S. Peirce, N.B. McGillicaddy and H. Syna (1992). Short term success in mediation: Its relationship to disputant and mediator behaviors and prior conditions. Journal of Conflict Resolution, 36: 546-572.

Chapter on concepts

Action

An action is here understood as an actor's intention, intention structure and manifestation. An action is contrasted to an event, which is evidence of events only to a limited extent within the actor's control.

Ambidextrous organizations. *Ambidextrous organizations* are organizations that have the ability to adapt to changes in external conditions while at the same time generating their own future by means of, among other things, performance improvement, growth and innovation (Duncan, 1976; O'Reilly & Tushman, 2004, 2006, 2011; Thota & Munir, 2011). In chapter 6, we have shown how ambidextrous organizations can be developed by HR departments.

In 2004, O'Reilly & Tushman expressed that ambidextrous organizations would constitute one of the major challenges for management in the global knowledge economy.

The findings of O'Reilly & Tushman (2004) were overwhelming. Regarding the launching of radical innovations, they found that none of the cross-functional or unsupported teams and only a quarter of the teams with functional designs were able to produce radical innovations. However, among the ambidextrous organizations, 90% were successful in producing radical innovations. Empirical research has shown that this type of organizational design is best for producing both incremental and radical innovations (Thora & Munir, 2011).

Asplund's motivation theory[2]. In brief, this theory can be described in the following way: *People are motivated by social responses* (Asplund, 2010: 221-229). The following statement may be said to be a central point made by Asplund's theory: *When people receive social responses, their level of activity increases.*

Asplund's motivation theory is consistent with North's action theory (ref. North's action theory). Understood in this way, it seems reasonable to connect the two theories in the statement: *People are motivated by the social responses rewarded by the institutional framework.*

Availability cascades. This refers to the idea that we are all controlled by the image of reality created by the media, because this image is easy to retrieve from memory.

Availability proposition. This may be expressed as follow: The more easily information enters into our consciousness, the greater the likelihood that we will have confidence in that information. In other words, we believe more in the type of information that is available in memory than the information that is not so readily available.

---

[2] Asplund's motivation theory, a term we use here, is based on Asplund's research..

Behavioural perspective. This perspective focuses on the behaviour of employees as an explanation for the relationship between business strategy and the results obtained.

Boudon-Coleman diagram. This research methodology was developed by Mario Bunge (Bunge, 1978:76-79) based on insights made by the sociologists Boudon and Coleman. The purpose of the diagram is to show the relationship between the various levels, such as the macro and micro-levels. For instance, it is shown how changes at the macro-level, such as technological innovations in feudal society, can lead to increased income at the micro-level. However, it was shown that technological innovations could lead to weakening of the semi-feudal structures because dependency on land owners was reduced. Consequently, the landowners opposed such changes especially in the case of technological innovations, which Boudon has shown in his research (Boudon, 1981: 100). Coleman (Coleman, 1990: 7-12) started at the macro level, went to the individual level to find explanations and finally ended up at the macro level again.

An important purpose of Bunge's Boudon-Coleman diagram is to identify social mechanisms that maintain or change the phenomenon or problem under investigation (as mentioned above, in Boudon's analysis of semi-feudal society). Bunge's Boudon-Coleman diagram may be said to represent a "mixed strategy"; Bunge says the following: *When studying systems of any kind a) reduce them to their components (at some level) and the interaction among these, as well as among them and environmental items, but acknowledge and explain emergence* (see the chapter on concepts) *whenever it occurs, and b) approach systems from all pertinent sides and on all relevant levels, integrating theories or even research fields whenever unidisciplinarity proves to be insufficient* (Bunge, 1998:78). The purpose of this research strategy is to arrive at a deeper and more complete explanation of a system's behaviour.

Butterfly effects

Small, often haphazard and improbable variables potentially capable of having large-scale consequences for social systems and nature.

Calibration

Calibration is here understood as the basis conducive to change in one type of basic relationship to another, e.g. the transition from a symmetrical to a complementary relationship.

Capabilities. Capabilities are for an organization what abilities are for an individual.

An organizational capability may thus be defined as an organization's ability to perform a task, activity or process. Operational capabilities enable an organization to make money in the here and now (Winter, 2003: 991-995). Dynamic capabilities, as opposed to operational capabilities, are linked to processes of change. Change and innovation are at the centre of dynamic capabilities.

Simplified, one may say that organizational capabilities are something an organization does well compared to its competitors (Ulrich and Brockbank, 2005). These capabilities are intangible and therefore difficult for competitors to imitate (Wernerfelt, 1984).

Capta

Capta are data which is given a code and then rendering meaning for the observer.

Causal analysis

Making the functional relation and the sufficient conditions between actions and events visible.

Circular causality

Linear causal explanations are usually contrasted to teleological explanations. Linear causal explanations are normally related to the past, while teleological explanations are linked to the future. In circular causal explanations this distinction is abolished and included in a systemic-oriented integrated model, where cause, effect, and expectations are interrelated entities. All three elements are included in what we choose to call circular causal explanations. Only the relation between cause and effect is of a linear type. If the feed-back between effect and cause is introduced into the relation, a classic cybernetic structure will result. When expectation is coupled into the structure, we will have introduced a feed-forward mechanism, where the entire structure is to be regarded as a circular causal explanation.

Cohesive energy. In a social system cohesive energy is "the glue" that binds the system together. Cohesive energy is the social mechanisms that make the system durable. According to systemic thinking it is the relationships and actions that bind social systems together. The rationale is that relationships and the systems of relationships may be said to control human behaviour. Social systems are held together (in systemic thinking) by dynamic social relations (e.g. feelings, perceptions, norms) and social action (e.g. cooperation, solidarity, conflict and communication).

Communicative consciousness

Communicative consciousness is linked to various preconditions which must occur, referred to as the cybernetic situation. Communicative consciousness is an ideal claim on the communicating partner. The cybernetic situation is based on the following ideal claims which in turn affect the level of the communicative consciousness, depending on the extent to which the ideal claim is embedded in the dialogue. The ideal claims on the cybernetic situation are:

1. The listener listens without evaluating the other person's statement while he/she is speaking, i.e. the attention is focused around an asking contrasted to an answer-oriented attitude.

2. The parties implied pursue an open, free and mutual dialogue, where the master/slave relation is completely transcended.

3. The parties have complementarity as their starting point, i.e. a helping basic attitude, where unrestrained confidence prevails.

4. The actors know that any explanation is subjective and fragmented.

5. The parties involved in the communicative process understand that premises, suppositions, preconditions and motives must be made explicit, and that additionally, the focusing on moral/ethical results and consequences of scientific problems approaches and problem solutions are obvious entities.

6. The ability to see how one's communicative actions affect the other

party(ies) involved in the dialogues.

7. Never to use other people as means to reach own personal goals.

8. The only force in operation is the obligation to give argumentative reasons for one's statements, and in this way to validate the dialogue.

Co-creation. Co-creation involves working together to promote knowledge processes and innovation. If knowledge processes and innovation are essential for value creation in the knowledge society, co-creation is an important social mechanism for initiating, maintaining and strengthening these processes. The balance between competition and cooperation, embodied in the concept of co-creation, leads to constructive criticism and the necessary scope of knowledge that exists in the network so as to promote creativity and the innovative. Instead of a zero-sum situation, a positive-sum situation will be developed where everyone wins.

Collective blindness. Collective blindness may be said to be a form of collective arrogance, which results in irrational actions. Minor events slip under the radar, causing the system to not be fully aware of what is happening. Politicians' explanations why voters in a referendum vote contrary to what most of the power elite and the media advocated is an example of collective blindness.

Competence. Competence refers to knowledge, skills and attitudes.

Complementary relationship

The behaviour of actor B complements the behaviour of actor A. Complementary relationships are based on a basic trust among the actors in the relationship.

Core Competence. The concept was popular in the strategy literature of the 1990s. Core competence may be defined as: *"a bundle of skills and technologies that enable a company to provide a particular benefit to customers"* (Hamel & Prahalad, 1996:219). More recently, core competence as a concept has been given less attention in the research on dynamic capabilities, and now there is more focus on the concept of *fitness*. The term *evolutionary fitness* is also used in the research literature in connection with technology, quality, cost development, market development, innovation and competitive positioning (Helfat, et al, 2007: 7).

Creatura

The communicative world.

Data

Data is here understood as a set of terms which in themselves do not necessarily render meaning, but which are a representation in one code or another of certain terms. For data to turn into capta, the code must be understood by the observer.

Discontinuous innovations. These are innovations that change the premises of technology, markets, our mindset, and so on. We know that sooner or later discontinuous innovations will emerge in the future (Hewing, 2013).

Dynamic capabilities. Dynamic capabilities stem from the resource-based perspective and evolutionary thinking in strategy literature (Teece, 2013: 3-65; 82-113; Nelson and Winter, 1982). The dynamic perspective attempts to explain what promotes an organization's competitive position over time through innovation and growth (Teece, 2013: x).

The original thinking concerning dynamic capabilities may be related to Teece et al. (1997). These authors defined dynamic capabilities as *an organization's ability to create, develop and modify its internal and external expertise in order to address changes in the external world.*

Dynamic capabilities are now seen as all the organizational processes, not only internal and external expertise, that contribute to an organization's capacity to adapt to change while creating the organization's future.

Epistemology

By epistemology is here meant our way of thinking in terms of scientific problems.

Explicit knowledge. This is knowledge that can be digitized and communicated to others as information.

Evidence. This may be results, such as research results, that can be relied on. However, it is also important to be aware of the fact that other evidence may be available without having to refer to figures and quantities, such as evidence that emerges from observations and good judgment without the assessment being quantified. Evidence-based research is research results that are based on approved and accepted scientific research methods.

Emergent. An emergent occurs if something new turns up on one level that has not previously existed on the level below. With emergent we mean: *Let S be a system with composition A, i.e. the various components in addition to the way they are composed. If P is a property of S, P is emergent with regard to A, if and only if no components in A possess P; otherwise P is to be regarded as a resulting property with regards to A.* (Bunge, 1977:97).

Entrepreneurial spirit. The entrepreneurial spirit may be described as follows (Roddick, 2003: 106-107):

- The vision of something new and belief in this that is so strong that belief becomes reality.
- A touch of positive madness.
- The ability to stand out from the crowd.
- Creative tension bubbling over.
- Pathological optimism.
- To act before you know!
- Basic desire for change.
- Creative energy focused on ideas, not on explicit factual knowledge.
- Being able to tell the story you want to sell.

Feedback Giving the other person feedback, for instance with regard to their behaviour, attitudes, and the like, is the most important element in the area of interactive skills and emotional intelligence (Goleman, 1996; 2007). Analysis of feedback is a sure way to identify our strengths and then reinforce them (Wang, et al., 2003). Failure to give people feedback on their behavior in some contexts may even be considered immoral.

Feed-forward. Feed-forward is regarded here as an expectation mechanism. It seems reasonable to assume that our expectations influence our behaviour in the present. It is therefore important that we make explicit to ourselves the expectations we have of a situation. By making expectations explicit, we have a greater opportunity to learn from our experiences and thus improve our performance.

Feed-pre

Feed-pre is linked to the entities: Language, history, tradition and the epistemological hierarchy. Feed-pre is influential on the interpretation of information in feed-back processes, and is thus instrumental in establishing these.

Front line focus. This refers to those in the front line, i.e. in direct contact with customers, users, patients, students, etc. They have the greatest expertise, necessary information, and decision-making authority and are regarded as the most important resource in the organization because they are at the point where an organization's value creation occurs.

Global competence network. These competence networks may be divided into political, social, economic, technological and cultural patterns. It is when these five patterns interact that one may perceive the overall pattern. In the global knowledge economy it seems reasonable to assume that those who control this pattern set the conditions for economic development. These global competence networks will most likely make an impact on HR departments in companies competing for this kind of expertise in national markets.

Global competence networks are also emphasized as crucial for economic growth by OECD (2001), although they use the term *innovative clusters*. The purpose of innovative clusters and global competence networks is the development, dissemination and use of new ideas that promote wealth creation.

There is much to suggest that a greater degree of integration and cooperation between private and public sectors at the national and regional levels is an important prerequisite for initiating the innovative locomotive effect. The global competence networks are metaphorically the energy source that sustains the motion of this locomotive. It would be counterproductive to replace the locomotive once in motion. Conversely, the individual carriages of the locomotive (read: organizational level) can be changed depending on their competitive position. The individual passengers on the train create ideas and knowledge through the processes that may be called *creative chaos*. In this way we will arrive at a tripartite of the prerequisites for global competence networks. At the individual level, creative chaos occurs. At the organizational level, there will be creative destruction. At the social and global levels, creative collaboration takes place. These three processes create innovation and economic growth as an emergent, not as a *future perfectum*, i.e. a planned process with given results.

A prerequisite for the reasoning above is that tension and competition at one level requires collaboration at another level. Competition and cooperation are both necessary if one is to develop innovation and economic growth, in the same manner that stability and change are necessary for flexibility. Too much of the one (stability) leads to rigidity, and too much of the other (change) leads to chaos. Understood in this way, emergents cannot be planned.

Hamel's Law of Innovation. The "law" states that only between one and two of one thousand ideas become innovations in a market (Hamel, 2002; 2012). Therefore, an infostructure must be created to ensure that ideas are continuously produced in a business.

Hidden knowledge. Hidden knowledge is what we do not know we do not know. Kirzner (1982) says that hidden knowledge is possibly the most important knowledge domain of creativity, innovation and entrepreneurship.

History's "slow fields".

This refers to the fact that norms, values and actions tend to be in operation long after the functions, activities and processes that initially created them disappear, thus generating so-called *slow fields of history*. These norms, values and actions exist though they have no apparent function, contributing to maintaining a type of behaviour long after the type of behaviour is functional or meaningful[3]. For sociologists and historians it is important to determine whether norms and values have any function, or whether they are part of history's slow fields. By examining history's slow fields, it may be possible to provide better explanations for phenomena.

HR management. HR management is defined as HR practices at various levels (micro, meso, macro) for managing people in organizations.

HR management has been defined in many different ways. For instance, Boxall and Purcell (2003:1) define HR management as all those activities oriented towards managing relations between employees in an organization. This definition emphasizes the relational perspective. Later, they expanded their definition to include all the activities and processes that underpin an organization's value creation (Boxall and Purcell, 2010:29). On this basis, Armstrong defines the activities and processes that HR management should

---

[3] Asplund (1970: 55) refers to a similar phenomenon when he discusses Simmel. He points out that the norms that may have had a positive function during a historic phase become in a later phase dysfunctional.

engage in: *"HRM covers activities such as human capital management, knowledge management, organizational design and development, resource planning (recruitment, talent development), performance management, organizational learning, reward systems, relationships between employees, and employees' wellness."* (Armstrong, 2014:6). However, we believe Armstrong underestimates two essential areas of knowledge in his definition: the management of innovation processes, and change processes in organizations. Innovation and change are strongly emphasized in the global HRM Survey (White & Younger, 2013:35-39). Armstrong has included the ethical perspective in his Handbook for HRM (Armstrong, 2014a:95-105). Management of innovation processes and change processes in organizations is also highlighted and underlined by Wright et al. (2011: 5) in their description of HRM. However, it must also be said that Armstrong discusses innovation (Armstrong, 2014:145-155), but not in his process definition of HR management. Innovation and change processes are also emphasized by Ulrich et al. (2013). Brockbank (2013: 24) especially mentions these two processes as being important in the research model Ulrich et al. (2013) have developed through their empirical research over 25 years.

Implicit Knowledge. This is knowledge that is spread throughout an organization but not integrated.

Information

By information is here meant the human interpretation of capta.
Information input overload. This occurs when an individual, a team, an organization or a community receive more information than they can manage to process.

In a situation characterised by information input overload the following may occur (Miller, 1978: 123):

1. Designated tasks and responsibilities are left undone
2. Errors are made
3. Queues of information occur
4. Information is filtered out that should have been included
5. Abstract formulations are made when they should have been specific
6. Communication channels are overloaded, creating stress and tension in the system
7. Complex situations are shunned
8. Information is lumped together for processing

Each of the above eight points may result in a decrease in efficiency when the system is exposed to information input overload.

Information management

Information management is here regarded as strategic running and control of internal information an internal communication, in addition to external information and external communication, with or without the use of information technology, where increased organisational efficiency is the goal. The partial areas which both IRM and information management comprise are: Governance and control in organisations, innovation processes in terms of technique performance, technology and management, information & service, Business Intelligence System, information strategy, information and organisational change processes, communication and organisational learning. What separates IRM and information management, is that IRM is oriented towards the mentioned partial areas in relation to computer applications, whereas information management is linked to information processes, information type, and communication for the mentioned entities.

Information Resource Management (IRM)

By IRM we understand the integrated management of various applications of computer systems.
It may be said that the *info*structure has the same importance in the knowledge society as the *infra*structure had in the industrial society.

Infostructure. The infostructure concerns the processes that enable the development, transfer, analysis, storage, coordination and management of data, information and knowledge. The infostructure consists of eleven generic processes, as shown in Fig. 8 in this book. The eleven processes in the infostructure may be considered as nodes in a social network at different levels, for example team, organization, society, and region, all in the global space. Together, the eleven processes comprise the totality of the infostructure.

Intention structure

By intention structure is here meant premises, suppositions, preconditions, motives, goals, emotions, expectation, and will.

Innovation. Innovation is here understood as any idea, practice or material element, which is perceived as new for the person using it (Zaltman et al., 1973).

Ideas are seen as the smallest unit in the innovation process (Hamel, 2002; 2012). However, this refers to the ideas that are in process of development and not fully developed ideas. Before an idea can be characterized as innovative, it must prove to be beneficial to somebody, i.e. the market must accept the idea and apply it. Consequently, the creative process of innovation is here understood as the benefit it has for a market (Amabile, 1990; Johannessen, et al., 2001: 25). Thus, it is not sufficient that an idea is new for it to be considered an innovation. An idea may have a great degree of novelty, but if it is of no benefit to anybody in the market, then it has no innovative value.

Kaizen. This is a Japanese method, which means that an organization develops systems for organized improvement (Maurer, 2012).

Knowledge. The definition of knowledge used here is *the systematization and structuring of information for one or more goals or purposes.*

Knowledge worker. A knowledge worker has been described by the OECD as *a person whose primary task is to generate and apply knowledge*, rather than to provide services or produce physical products (OECD, 2000 a, b, c, d, e; 2001). This may be understood as a *formal definition* of a knowledge worker.

This definition does not restrict knowledge workers to creative fields, as is the case with, for example, Mosco and McKercher (2007: vii–xxiv). The

OECD definition also allows for the fact that a knowledge worker may perform routine tasks. The definition also does not limit the type of work performed by knowledge workers to tasks relating to creative problem-solving strategies, unlike the definition provided by Reinhardt et al. (2011).

Knowledge enterprise. This is an enterprise that has knowledge as its most significant output. It is perhaps helpful to think of the process *input - process - output* to separate industrial enterprises from knowledge enterprises. Much knowledge and skills are needed to produce high-tech products such as computers, and there are also many knowledge workers involved in this process. However, the majority of products produced today are high-tech industrial products, and although such products require very skilled knowledge in the production process, they are nevertheless output-industrial products.

On the other hand, law firms, consulting firms and universities are examples of knowledge enterprises.

Knowledge management. Management of knowledge resources in an organization. These resources may be explicit knowledge, implicit knowledge, tacit knowledge and hidden knowledge.

Locomotive effect. This refers to something that generates and then reinforces an activity or development.

Message

The message is the minimum entity in the type of communication being discussed here. Every message can be said to consist of three parts. These are:

1. The information part, which can be both implicit and explicit in a message.

2. The influence part, which is the intentional and influencing part of a message. The influence part is closely linked to the power concept, which in turn could be linked to the master/slave distinction.

3. The relationship part. Here a distinction has been made between two archetypes of relationships, namely the symmetrical and the complementary.

Modularization. An extreme fragmentation of the production process in the global knowledge economy. Production is fragmented and distributed according to the following logic: Costs – quality – competence – design –

innovation.

Modular flexibility. The modulization of value creation. Modular flexibility may best be understood as the globalization of production processes, and extreme specialization of work processes with a focus on core processes.

Necessary and sufficient conditions. It may often be appropriate to divide conditions or premises into *necessary conditions* and *sufficient conditions*. Necessary conditions must be present to trigger an action, but these may not be sufficient. The sufficient conditions must also be present to trigger the action.

Non-knowledge

In the process from data via capta to information and knowledge, we continuously select out something. What we select out in this process constitutes non-knowledge.

North's action theory[4]. This action theory may be expressed in the following statement: *People act on the basis of a system of rewards as expressed in the norms, values, rules and attitudes in the culture (the institutional framework)* (North, 1990; 1993). North's action theory is also consistent with Asplund's motivation theory (ref. Asplund's motivation theory).

---

[4] North's action theory is a term we use here based on North's research.

Pleroma

The dead/ raw physical world

Pre-comprehension

Pre comprehension contains the processes constituting understanding. Pre comprehension thus becomes the foundation of understanding. Exactly by going behind the questions and statements, pre comprehension itself can be obviated. One way of achieving this is to use the ontological questioning process.

Prestructures

Three pre-structures exist:

1. An understanding of the totality of a subject matter.

2. An initial understanding of what type of phenomenon we are faced with.

3. The fact that we have pre-concepts regarding a phenomenon.

Primary task. An organization's primary task is what the system is designed to do.

Proposition. This is an overarching hypothesis. It says something about the relationship between several variables. A proposition relates to a hypothesis in the same way the main research problem relates to research questions.

Punctuation. By punctuation (Bateson, 1972:292-293) a distinction is drawn between cause and effect; this is done with a clear motive in mind. A causality is thus created which does not actually exist in the real world, and one is then free to discuss the effects of this cause which has been created through a process of punctuation.

A sequence of a process is selected, and then bracketed. In this way, we delimit what is punctuated from the rest of the process. Figuratively, we may imagine this as a circle that is divided into small pieces; one piece of the circle is then selected and folded out into a straight line. This results in the creation of an artificial beginning and end. This beginning and end of course cannot exist in a circle, but only through the process of punctuation.

Recursive thinking.

Recursive thinking here means that circular causality must be explained at various logical levels in the system(s) we choose to study. These various logical levels are then inter-dependent and must ultimately be viewed contextual in order to render meaning for the observer.

Sensitising concepts

Sensitising concepts are concepts which are not definitive or operationalized, but which are subject to constant change. Sensitising concepts are based on proximity to experiences regarding the problem area in question.

Social laws. Social laws constitute a pattern of a unique type. They are systemic and connected to a system of knowledge, and cannot change without the facts they represent also being changed (Bunge, 1983; 1983a). The main differences between a statement of a law and other statements are:

1. Law statements are general.

2. Law statements are systemic, i.e. they are related to the established system of knowledge.

3. Law statements have been verified through many studies.

A pattern may be understood as variables that are stable over a specific period of time. A social law is created when an observer gains insight into the pattern. By gaining such insight, we can also predict parts of behaviour or at least develop a rough estimate within a short period of time.

Social laws are further related to specific social systems, both in time and space. However, this does not represent any objection to social laws, because this is also true of natural laws (although these have a longer time span and are of a more general nature).

Social mechanism. Robert Merton (1967) brought the notion of social mechanisms into sociology, although we can find rudiments of this in both Weber – with the Protestant ethic as an explanation for the emergence of capitalism in Europe – and in Durkheim, who uses society as an explanation for a rising suicide rate. For Merton, social mechanisms are the building blocks of *middle range theories*. He defines social mechanisms as *social processes having designated consequences for designated parts of the social structure* (Merton, 1968:43). In the 1980s and 1990s, Jon Elster developed a new notion of the role of social mechanisms in sociology (Elster, 1983;1989). Hedstrom and Swedberg write that, *the advancement of social theory calls for an analytical approach that systematically seeks to explicate the social mechanisms that generate and explain observed associations between events* (Hedstrøm & Swedberg, 1998:1).

It is one thing to point out connections between phenomena. It is something quite different to point out satisfactory explanations for these relationships, which is what social mechanisms accomplish. A social mechanism tells us what will happen, how it will happen and why it will happen (Bunge, 1967). Social mechanisms are primarily analytical constructs which cannot necessarily be observed; in other words, they are epistemological, not ontological. However, social mechanisms are observable in their consequences. An intention can be a social mechanism of action. We cannot observe an intention, but we can interpret it in light of the consequences manifested through an action. Preferences can also function as a social mechanism for economic behaviour. We cannot observe a person's preferences, but we can interpret them in the light of the behavioural consequences that manifest themselves. Social mechanisms are, understood in this way, analytical constructs, indicating connections between events (Hernes, 1998).

Bunge says: *"... a social mechanism is a process in a concrete system, such that it is capable of being about or preventing some change in the system as a whole or in some of its subsystems"* (Bunge, 1997:414). By 'social mechanism' here we mean those activities that promote/inhibit social processes in relation to a specific problem / phenomenon.

Material resources and technology are social mechanisms of the economic subsystem; power is a social mechanism of the political subsystem; fundamental norms and values are a social mechanism of the cultural subsystem; and human relationships are a social mechanism of the social subsystem. These system-specific social mechanisms interact with each other to achieve certain goals, maintain these systems, or to avoid certain undesirable conditions in the system or the outside world.

The difficulty of discovering social mechanisms and distinguishing them from processes may be partly explained by the fact that social mechanisms are also processes (Bunge, 1997:414). For the application of social mechanisms, see the Boudon-Coleman diagram.

Social system. From a systemic perspective, social systems can be conceptual or concrete. Theories and analytical models are examples of conceptual systems. Further, social systems are *composed of people and their artifacts* (Bunge, 1996:21). Social systems are held together (in systemic reasoning) by **dynamic social relations** (such as emotions, interpretations, norms, etc.) and **social actions** (such as, cooperation, solidarity, conflict and communication, etc.). None of the social actions have precedence in the systemic interpretation of social systems, such as conflict in the case of Marx, and solidarity in the case of Durkheim.

Spontaneous intuition

By spontaneous intuition we here mean the sudden, haphazard component which causes the researcher to alter his strategy in the immediate confrontation with the research object. This implies that e.g. a completed interview guide must give way to factors which may occur at the spur of the moment between a researcher and the social system he/she investigates.

The precondition here is that it is the transcension of knowledge which comes first, not the inter subjectivity of the instrument.

Staccato-behaviour (erratic behaviour). If organizations introduce too many change processes in succession too quickly, a phenomenon may occur called "staccato-behaviour".

If an organization does not deal with this appropriately, it seems reasonable to assume that workers will become tired, burnt-out and de-motivated. Perhaps most damaging to business, employees will lose focus on their primary task - what the business is designed to do. In addition, businesses will often experience that this leads to an increasing degree of opportunistic behaviour (Ulrich, 2013a:260).

Strategic HR management. Strategic HR management is defined in this book as: *The choices an HR department makes with regard to human resources for the purposes of achieving the organization's goals.* This is analogous to the view of Storey et al. (2009:3) and consistent with the definition we employ of HR management. This means that strategic HR management must be focused on the *micro, meso* and *macro-levels*.

There are many definitions of strategic HR management. For instance, *use of human resources in order to achieve lasting competitive advantages for the business*

(Mathis and Jackson, 2008:36); *management of the employees, expressed through management philosophy, policy and praxis* (Torrington et al., 2005:28); *development of a consistent practices in order to support the strategic goals of the business* (Mello, 2006:152); *a complex system with the following characteristics: vertical integration, horizontal integration, efficiency, partnership* (Schuler and Jackson, 2005).

Systemic thinking. Systemic thinking makes a distinction between the epistemological sphere (Bunge, 1985), the ontological sphere (Bunge, 1983), the axiological sphere (Bunge, 1989, 1996) and the ethical sphere (Bunge, 1989). Systemic thinking makes a clear distinction between intention and behaviour. Intention is something that should be *understood*, while behaviour is something that should be *explained*. To understand an intention we must study the historical factors, situations and contexts, as well as the expectation mechanisms. Behaviour must be explained with respect to the context, relationships and situation it unfolds in. What implication does the distinction between intention and behavior have for the study of social systems?

Interpretation of meaning is an important part of the *intention aspect* in the distinction. Explanation and prediction become an essential part of the *behavioral aspect* of the distinction.

In systemic thinking it is the link between the interpretation of meaning and explanation, and prediction, which provides historical and social sciences with practical strength. By making a distinction between intention and behaviour, the historical and the social sciences are interpretive, explanatory and predictive projects. According to systemic thinking, many of the contradictions in the historical and social sciences spring from the fact that a distinction is not made between intention and behaviour. The problem of the historical and social sciences is that the actors who are studied have both intentions and they also exercise types of behaviour; however, this isn't problematic as long as we make a distinction between intention and behaviour. By simultaneously introducing the distinction between intention and behaviour, systemic thinking has made it possible to identify, for instance, partial explanations from each of two main epistemological positions, namely, the naturalists and anti-naturalists (Johannessen & Olaisen, 2005; 2006), and synthesize these explanations into new knowledge.

Systemic thinking emphasizes circular causal processes, also called *interactive causal processes*, in addition to linear causal processes (Johannessen, 1996; 1997). Systemic thinking argues that to understand objective social facts, one must examine the subjective aspects of these. In systemic thinking, objective social facts exist, but they are often more difficult to grasp than facts in the natural world, because social facts are often influenced by expectations, emotions, prejudices, ideology and economic and social interests. *"Aspect-seeing"* is thus a way of approaching these social facts.

Emergents are central to systemic thinking. A pattern behind the problem or phenomenon is always sought in systemic investigations. Patterns may be revealed by studying the underlying processes that constitute a phenomenon or problem, *and the search for pattern is what scientific research is all about* (Bunge, 1996:42).

According to systemic thinking it is a misconception to say that the facts are social constructions. The misunderstanding involves confusing our *concepts* concerning facts and our *hypotheses* about the facts together with the facts. Our concepts and hypotheses are mental constructs. The facts, however, are not mental constructs. Social need, for instance, is not a social fact; it is a mental construct of, for instance, starvation. Starvation is a social fact. Social need is a mental or social construction. Not being able to read is a social fact. Illiteracy is, however, a social construction.

A *symbol* should symbolize something, just as a *concept* should delineate something. A *hypothesis* should explain something or express something about relationships. A conceptual *model* should say something about the relationships between concepts. A *theory* should say something about relationships between propositions. Physical or social facts are untouched by all these mental constructions. That one can through constructs change social facts, or that social facts are changed as a social consequence of using constructs, is neither original nor new.

The aim of theoretical research, according to the systemic position, is the construction of systems, i.e. theories (Bunge, 1974: v). The order in systemic research is thus: Theory - Analysis - Synthesis.

In the methodological sphere, the systemic position has its main focus on relationships, both in terms of concrete things, ideas and knowledge. Consequently, systemic thinking encourages interdisciplinary and multidisciplinary approaches to problems or phenomena.

The systemic position thus attempts to bridge the gap between methodological individualism and methodological collectivism, which is considered the classic controversy in historical- and social sciences.

The perceptions that an observer has about social systems will influence his/her actions, regardless of whether the perceptions are true or fallacious. Systemic investigations start, therefore, writes Bunge *from individuals embedded in a society that preexists them and watch how their actions affect society and alter it* (Bunge, 1996:241). The study of social systems from a systemic perspective for these reasons always includes the triad: actors - observers - social systems.

The observer tries to uncover a system's composition, environment and structure. Then the actors' subjective perception of composition, environment and structure are examined. In other words, both the subjective and objective aspects are studied. When we wish to study changes in social systems, from a systemic point of view, we have to examine the social mechanisms (drivers) that influence changes; both internal and external social mechanisms must be identified. This study takes place within the four subsystems: the economic, political, cultural and relational. According to systemic thinking, social changes occur along seven axes:

1. As an *expectation* of new relationships, values, power constellations, technologies and distribution of material resources.
2. As a result of our *beliefs* (mental models) about relationships, values, power constellations, technical and material resources.
3. As a result of *psychological elements*, such as: irritation, crisis, discomfort, unsatisfactory life, unworthy life, loss of well-being, etc.
4. As a result of *communication* in and between systems.

5. As a result of an *understanding of connections* (contextual understanding).

6. As a result of learning and new *self-knowledge*.

7. As a result of *new ideas* and ways of thinking.

Historiography, from a systemic perspective, has one clear goal: to investigate what happened, where it happened, when it happened, how it happened, why it happened, and with what results.

Systemic assumptions related to historiography and social sciences may be expressed in the following (Bunge 1998:263):

a. The past has existed.

b. Parts of the past can be known.

c. Every uncovering of the past will be incomplete.

d. New data, techniques, and systemizations and structuring will reveal new aspects of the past.

e. Historical knowledge is developed through new data, discoveries, hypotheses and approaches.

In systemic thinking if changes are to take place, then the material will sometimes be given precedence; at other times, ideology, ideas and thinking are given precedence. In other contexts, there is a systemic link between the material and ideas that is needed to bring about changes. In such contexts, it is difficult and irrelevant to say what is the primary driver, i.e. the material or ideas; this would be on par with discussing what came first, the chicken or the egg.

The processes that drive social change, according to a systemic perspective, are the interaction between the economic, political, relational and cultural subsystems. In some situations, one of these four perspectives will prevail, whereas in others it will be one or more of the four subsystems that are the drivers of social change. In many cases, it is precisely the interaction between the four subsystems that leads to social changes.

In this context the systemic perspective may be described by saying that material conditions/energy, such as economic relationships, may provide the ground from which ideologies develop, but that these ideologies in return influence the development of the material. Whether material conditions / energy or ideology comes first is often determined by a historiographical punctuation process (Bateson, 1972:163).

The systemic perspective balances historical materialism and historical idealism. It assumes that overall social changes are the result of economic, political, social and cultural factors, in addition to the interaction between material conditions / energy and ideas. Furthermore, a systemic perspective views any society as being interwoven into its surroundings (Bunge, 1998:

275). When a historian considers a historical situation – such as the massacre in Van in April 1915 – from this perspective then he is trying *to throw light upon the internal working of a past culture and society* (Stone, 1979: 19).

The systemic position attempts to view the relevant event in a larger context, in order to find *the patterns which combine* (Bateson, 1972:273-274), because *change depends upon feedback loop* (Bateson, 1972:274). Bunge says about this position: *By placing the particular in a sequence, adopting a broad perspective the systemist overcomes the idiographic/ nomothetic duality, …, as well as the concomitant narrative/ structural opposition* (Bunge 1998:275). This means, metaphorically, that the systemic researcher uses a microscope, telescope and a helicopter to investigate patterns over time.

Systemic research strategy is a *zig-zagging between the micro-meso and macro levels* (Bunge, 1998:277). Through a systemic research strategy the researcher has ample opportunities to use a Boudon-Coleman diagram.

Systemic thinking examines four types of changes[5].

<u>Type I change</u> concerns individuals who change history, such as Genghis Khan, Hitler, Stalin, Mao Zedong, etc.

<u>Type II change</u> concerns groups of people acting together who change

---

[5] The four types of changes are related to Bateson's (1972:279-309) work on different types of learning, especially those discussed in his chapter *Logical types of learning and communication.*

history. Examples of Type II change include the invasion of the Roman Empire by peoples from the north; and the Ottoman expansion into the Balkans between the late 1400s and when the Ottoman Empire was pushed back partly due to nationalist liberation movements in the early 1900s.

<u>Type III change</u> include changes in history that are caused by natural disasters, such as the volcanic eruption that destroyed Pompeii. Climate change may also be said to an example of a type III change.

<u>Type IV change</u> involves a total change in the way of thinking, such as the emergence of new religions, like Islam, or a new political ideology, such as Marxism.

The systemic researcher attempts to explore the relationship between the four types of changes. A single event is in itself not necessarily of special interest to the systemic researcher; rather, the focus is on the *system of events* of which the single event is a part.

All the social sciences are used in the systemic position to seek insight, understanding and to explain a phenomenon or problem.

Symmetrical relationship

When actor A does something it is likely that actor B will do more of the same. A symmetrical relationship is based on mistrust and suspicion among the actors.

Tacit knowledge. Knowledge that is difficult to communicate to others as information. It is also very difficult, if at all possible, to digitize.

"The Context of Solution"

Moral/ethical results and consequence considerations in respect of scientific problem approaches and solutions at the local level are included in what we choose to denote as "The Context of Solution". Science is in CS regarded as the totality of the three contexts: "The Context of Discovery", "The Context of Justification" and "The Context of Solution".

The epistemological hierarchy

Our way of thinking in terms of scientific problems is in this concept regarded as a hierarchical structure in the following logical order: Meta-theory, theory, model and method. The superior levels influence the subordinate levels. This implies that in order to make our way of thinking explicit, all logical levels must be clarified for us as researchers.

The naturalist erroneous inference.

This is "The Mainstream Science" demonstration that it is directly wrong for science to infer from is to should. By introducing this entity "The Mainstream Science" has coupled moral/ ethical result and consequence considerations out of the scientific domain.

The objectivist position

Here we think of scientists with the notion that they can reflect circumstances in nature and social systems by means of honing specific methods and techniques. To the objectivistic school belong positivists, logical positivists, neo-positivists, empiricists, logical empiricists and empirical analysts. The contrast to the objectivistic school is the contrustivistic school, which is based on the notion that reality is constructed socially by the observers.

The ontological questioning process.

This is a strategy aimed at the penetration beyond questions and statements in order to uncover premises, suppositions and prerequisites immanent in the questions and statements. The strategy consists of five elements:

1. Let us look at the following areas.

2. Let us look at the questions and statements used in the area in question.

3. Let us go behind the questions and look if they are constructed with the answers implicit in the questions.

4. Let us edit the questions so that no answers are implicit in the questions.

5. Let us go behind the statements and see what questions they answer.

Point 5 then leads back to point 3 and then to point 4.

The knowledge-based perspective. The knowledge-based perspective is defined here as creating, expanding and modifying internal and external competencies to promote what the organization is designed to do (Grant, 2003: 203).

The paradox of objectivity

The paradox of objectivity occurs in the following process:

1. First the social reality is generated.

2. Then action is taken to uncover the underlying reality.

3. Finally we adapt to what we originally have been instrumental in creating.

Only when the three processes are carried out by one system is this paradox made visible.

The perceptual filter.

The perceptual filter consists of three elements:

1. Generalisation, i.e. the abstraction leaps we make from data in the problem area.

2. Selection, i.e. the selective process conducive to our attention to the individual dimensions in our experience and our selection-out of others.

3. Biasing, i.e. the process leading to the selection of some dimensions in the object field and the disregard for others.

The shadow filter.

The shadow filter indicates the distinction between the description and the described, i.e. between the descriptive statements about the object system, the object field, the problem area etc., and these entities. The shadow filter consists of three entities which mutually affect each other. These are:

Prestructures, the perceptive filter, and descriptive statements about the object system, object field, problem area etc.

The theory of science

The theory of science is here regarded as the science of the individual sciences. The theory of science is a meta- theory for the individual sciences. This meta-theory influences the individual sciences. The theory of science is in the project before us meant to encompass:

The philosophy of science, The history of science, The sociology of science and the psychology of science, i.e. that the four entities are subsumed under the concept scientific theory.

The resource-based perspective. This perspective can be defined as the structuring and systematization of the organization's internal *resources* so it is difficult for competitors to copy them.

Theory. Here understood as a system of propositions (Bunge, 1974: v).

Third order cybernetics

Third order cybernetics is about the entities:

Relationship, communication, meaning, and interpretation processes. Third order cybernetics is the cybernetics of relationships between two or more observing systems. First order cybernetics is the cybernetic of the observed system. Second order cybernetics is the cybernetics of the observing system.

Trialectic.

Trialectic emphasises patterns, accelerating change, information explosion and environmental limitations. The focus in trialectic is on change and the change mechanisms in trial ethics are attraction variables in a system through a pattern of relations. The axioms for trialectic are :

1. The axiom based on advancement by rushes, i.e. changes occur in rushes from one state to the other.

2. The circulation axiom, i.e. opposite poles do not necessarily represent differences, but the one embodies the germ of the other.

3. The attraction axiom, i.e. active variables are attracted by attractive variables, which again affect the active variables.

An approach to a scientific problem in creatura can be conducted by means of trialectic in the following manner:

1. Seek for variables (C) which have attractive effect on other variables.

2. Seek for variables (D) which are active when actions are performed.

3. Seek for results manifested as a result of C and D.

4. Seek for functions operating in C and D.

5. Seek for relations and patterns separating and joining C and D.

Zappfe's paradox

You go down by what is your strength.

Index

A

A burning desire, 125
Anchoring, 102, 109, 111, 115
Attention, 48
attentional redeployment, 129
attitude, 24, 43, 54, 55, 72, 84, 87, 90, 121, 149, 150, 151, 152, 153, 154, 156, 157, 164, 165, 168, 169, 170, 171, 173, 174, 175, 176, 177, 179, 180, 181, 182, 184, 185, 187, 195
attitudes, v, 14, 24, 54, 55, 61, 72, 148, 149, 150, 151, 152, 153, 154, 155, 157, 158, 161, 162, 163, 164, 165, 166, 167, 169, 170, 171, 172, 173, 174, 175, 176, 178, 180, 183, 184, 185, 197, 200, 212
autopoietic, 50
Availability, 43, 90, 102, 104, 109, 186, 190

B

behaviour, 9, 16, 30, 35, 36, 48, 53, 56, 58, 118, 123, 127, 128, 129, 130, 134, 136, 149, 154, 160, 164, 166, 167, 168, 169, 171, 172, 173, 175, 176, 177, 178, 191, 192, 194, 197, 200, 201, 204, 215, 217, 219, 220, 221
belief system, 155
burning desire, 131, 133, 134, 135, 136, 139

C

certainty effect, 94, 95, 96, 98, 107

character, 124, 136
cognitive dissonance, 19, 39, 59, 83, 173
commitment, 59, 73, 95, 96, 110
communication, 7, 8, 11, 13, 14, 15, 16, 18, 38, 42, 45, 46, 51, 128, 149, 154, 161, 175, 182, 194, 207, 211, 218, 224, 227, 233
competence, 78, 79, 80, 119, 121, 123, 131, 197, 201, 202, 212
confidence, 15, 55, 60, 69, 76, 77, 78, 79, 105, 121, 160, 161, 190, 195
conflicts, 8, 9, 14
connection, 13, 15, 18, 45, 54, 80, 112, 170, 197
connotations, 52
context, iv, 7, 9, 10, 11, 12, 17, 19, 20, 21, 22, 23, 25, 26, 27, 28, 29, 31, 32, 33, 34, 35, 36, 54, 68, 80, 95, 96, 101, 105, 119, 130, 136, 142, 151, 168, 169, 171, 175, 176, 220, 226, 227
cybernetic, 122, 194, 233

D

decision, 15, 27, 35, 39, 40, 49, 51, 60, 67, 74, 82, 92, 99, 100, 110, 112, 114, 156, 201
definitions, 8, 14, 46, 121, 149, 220
differences, 9, 20, 22, 88, 125, 167, 215, 234
disputants, 11
distortions, 18

E

Emergent, 199
emotions, 33, 34, 127, 130, 163, 208,

218, 222
endurance, v, 116, 117, 130, 131, 134, 135, 136, 137, 138
erratic behavior, 102, 109
expectation, 53, 54, 55, 94, 95, 109, 164, 194, 201, 208, 220, 224
expectations, 10, 13, 23, 25, 53, 54, 55, 97, 99, 107, 109, 119, 121, 124, 164, 165, 175, 194, 201, 222
experiences, 10, 16, 17, 18, 19, 25, 68, 98, 104, 128, 135, 136, 150, 152, 156, 158, 174, 201, 215
explanation, 18, 33, 59, 62, 63, 64, 65, 67, 68, 93, 94, 171, 191, 192, 194, 195, 216, 221
extreme attitudes, 153

F

facial expressions, 150, 151
Feed-forward, 201

G

GRIT, 124, 125, 126

H

Heuristic, iv, v, 66, 102, 109, 111
heuristic assessments, 102, 110
hypothesis, 26, 43, 73, 81, 91, 187, 214, 222

I

inconsistent, 96
influence, v, 10, 12, 13, 18, 19, 26, 30, 34, 52, 61, 67, 79, 80, 81, 89, 108, 116, 130, 148, 150, 152, 153, 156, 158, 159, 166, 174, 175, 183, 188, 201, 211, 223, 224, 226, 229
information, iv, 7, 8, 9, 10, 11, 12, 13, 14, 15, 16, 17, 19, 22, 23, 24, 25, 26, 27, 28, 29, 30, 31, 32, 34, 35, 36, 37, 45, 46, 47, 48, 49, 50, 51, 52, 53, 54, 55, 56, 57, 58, 59, 61, 62, 64, 65, 66, 67, 68, 69, 71, 72, 73, 74, 75, 76, 77, 78, 79, 80, 81, 87, 89, 92, 96, 98, 100, 101, 102, 103, 104, 105, 107, 109, 110, 111, 119, 153, 155, 156, 157, 158, 159, 160, 161, 162, 163, 165, 181, 187, 190, 199, 201, 206, 207, 208, 209, 211, 212, 229, 233
interaction, 9, 11, 13, 21, 42, 53, 81, 86, 98, 128, 130, 164, 192, 226
interpretation, 11, 46, 47, 63, 68, 81, 201, 206, 218, 221, 233
isolation effect, 96, 98, 107

K

knowledge, 7, 8, 13, 14, 17, 25, 26, 31, 45, 46, 47, 48, 49, 50, 55, 61, 68, 69, 73, 79, 81, 82, 84, 86, 103, 104, 107, 111, 120, 121, 125, 150, 156, 157, 158, 175, 189, 196, 197, 199, 200, 202, 203, 205, 207, 208, 209, 210, 212, 215, 219, 221, 223, 225, 231

M

mastery, 116, 117, 123, 125, 138, 139
mechanism, 66, 67, 194, 196, 201, 216, 217
memory, 18, 19, 29, 66, 67, 68, 75, 85, 104, 105, 110, 111, 153, 156, 163, 179, 187, 190
message, 7, 8, 15, 45, 47, 51, 52, 62, 65, 159, 161, 175, 187, 211
Misinformation, 75, 163
model, iv, 7, 11, 12, 17, 21, 31, 32, 37, 41, 51, 52, 54, 78, 79, 80, 87, 96, 119, 122, 139, 154, 155, 164, 176, 194, 205, 222, 229
Moral courage, 126

N

Negotiation, 8, 9, 39, 41, 42, 88, 95, 98, 99, 102, 104, 106, 112, 184
negotiation theory, 9, 11

O

OECD, 202, 210
opportunities, 31, 95, 99, 100, 107, 147, 227
opportunity, 96, 98, 99, 132, 135, 201
organization, 92, 99, 102, 108, 119, 132, 136, 139, 188, 192, 193, 198, 201, 204, 205, 206, 208, 209, 211, 213, 219, 231, 233

P

perception, 7, 9, 26, 44, 45, 73, 91, 101, 110, 120, 128, 156, 180, 224
Perseverance, 125
phenomenon, 8, 9, 18, 19, 22, 23, 25, 29, 45, 48, 49, 53, 64, 68, 69, 70, 72, 74, 75, 77, 79, 100, 162, 163, 164, 191, 204, 213, 217, 219, 222, 228
positive psychology, 127, 143, 144, 145, 146
positive thinking, 123
possession, 56
possibility, 21, 23, 29, 92, 94, 96, 97, 149, 152, 153, 174
practical, 19, 36, 46, 95, 97, 112, 116, 148, 156, 221
pragmatics, 46, 48, 49, 50, 51
problem, 8, 9, 12, 13, 14, 16, 18, 19, 20, 22, 23, 25, 28, 34, 35, 36, 47, 48, 49, 59, 85, 91, 112, 154, 174, 191, 195, 210, 214, 215, 217, 221, 222, 228, 229, 231, 232, 234
problem-solving, 34, 210
procedures, 8, 47, 67
processes, iv, 7, 10, 12, 14, 15, 18, 25, 36, 39, 48, 51, 53, 58, 63, 68, 71, 72, 74, 80, 84, 92, 94, 98, 99, 115, 119, 130, 150, 151, 155, 157, 162, 178, 180, 181, 185, 187, 193, 196, 198, 201, 202, 204, 207, 208, 212, 213, 216, 217, 218, 219, 221, 222, 226, 231, 233
punktueringsprosessen, 214, 226

R

reappraisal, 130
reflection effect, 95, 96, 98, 107
relationship, 9, 12, 15, 22, 44, 45, 77, 78, 91, 126, 128, 157, 158, 165, 166, 167, 169, 172, 180, 187, 188, 191, 192, 197, 211, 214, 228
Resistance to change, 96, 113
Risk, 92, 107
risk aversion, 103, 108
Rumours, 53

S

Self-discipline, 126
self-efficacy, 121, 123
self-esteem, 119, 120, 121, 122, 124, 128, 141, 144, 147
self-image, 116, 117, 118, 119, 120, 127, 128, 135
self-regulation, v, 121, 127, 128, 129, 130, 141
situation, 7, 9, 10, 12, 13, 14, 15, 16, 17, 19, 20, 21, 25, 30, 31, 32, 33, 34, 35, 36, 50, 53, 56, 57, 60, 66, 67, 77, 92, 93, 94, 95, 96, 99, 100, 105, 106, 109, 128, 129, 135, 157, 160, 161, 165, 194, 196, 201, 206, 220, 227
social reality, 13, 17, 231
statement, 22, 56, 60, 108, 162, 173, 190, 195, 212, 215
strategies, 23, 56, 123, 129, 175, 176, 210

strategy, 26, 47, 48, 49, 51, 54, 57, 60, 61, 62, 63, 64, 66, 67, 68, 69, 70, 72, 73, 74, 77, 79, 80, 81, 86, 108, 129, 131, 135, 151, 191, 192, 197, 198, 207, 218, 227, 230

structure, 12, 13, 15, 22, 23, 46, 148, 154, 159, 179, 180, 181, 188, 189, 194, 208, 216, 224, 229

success, 23, 44, 91, 95, 102, 109, 125, 126, 139, 141, 188

system, 8, 30, 31, 32, 46, 47, 49, 50, 51, 54, 72, 74, 81, 100, 111, 120, 155, 157, 158, 173, 175, 176, 192, 194, 196, 199, 206, 212, 213, 215, 217, 218, 219, 220, 224, 228, 231, 232, 233

T

The anchor effect, 102, 104
The availability proposition, 105, 109
theory, v, 9, 11, 15, 19, 35, 39, 59, 60, 63, 71, 81, 83, 84, 90, 91, 92, 93, 94, 96, 97, 98, 100, 101, 103, 110, 112, 114, 115, 123, 124, 129, 140, 141, 151, 162, 172, 173, 177, 178, 180, 181, 190, 212, 216, 222, 229, 232

transform, 21, 23, 25, 29, 33, 36, 73
Type I change, 227
Type I-endring, 228
Type II change, 227
Type III change, 228
Type IV change, 228
typologies, 30, 53, 55, 56, 166

U

V

value, iv, 15, 16, 26, 30, 31, 32, 33, 54, 55, 72, 80, 87, 113, 164, 168, 169, 171, 196, 201, 204, 209, 212

W

win-lose, 20, 21, 23, 25, 27, 29, 33, 35, 36
win-win, 7, 11, 19, 20, 21, 23, 25, 27, 29, 33, 34, 35, 36, 109

Ø

About the Author

Jon-Arild Johannessen holds a Master of Science from Oslo University in History. He holds a Ph.D. from Stockholm University in Systemic thinking. He is currently professor (full) in Leadership, at Kristiania University College, Oslo and Nord University, Norway. He has been professor (full) in Innovation, at Syd-Danske University, Denmark. He has been professor (full) in Management at The Arctic University, Norway. At Bodø Graduate School of Business, Norway he had a professorship (full) in Information management. At Norwegian School of Management he has been professor in Knowledge Management.

www.ingramcontent.com/pod-product-compliance
Lightning Source LLC
Chambersburg PA
CBHW070228190526
45169CB00001B/125